A Classification of

North American

Biotic Communities

A Classification of
North American
Biotic Communities

David E. Brown

Frank Reichenbacher

Susan E. Franson

THE UNIVERSITY OF UTAH PRESS

SALT LAKE CITY

LIBRARY OF CONGRESS CATALOGING-IN-PUBLICATION DATA

Brown, David E. (David Earl), 1938–
    A classification of North American biotic communities / David E.
Brown, Frank Reichenbacher, Susan E. Franson.
      p.   cm.
    Includes bibliographical references (p.   ).
    ISBN 0-87480-562-7 (alk. paper)
    1. Biotic communities—North America—Classification.
I. Reichenbacher, Frank, 1955– . II. Franson, Susan E., 1953– .
III. Title.
QH102.B76 1998   97-53161
577.8'2'097—DC21

To M.D.F. (Nick) Udvardy

friend, mentor, and the inspiration for this book

Contents

Figures

Tables

Acknowledgments

We wish to express our gratitude to Tony Burgess, Biosphere II, Oracle, Arizona; Russell Davis, University of Arizona, Tucson; Michael Jennings, Fish and Wildlife Cooperative Research Unit and Office of Biological Services, Moscow, Idaho; Thomas R. Loveland, U.S. Geological Survey, Sioux Falls, South Dakota; W. L. Minckley, Arizona State University, Tempe; James M. Omernik, U.S. Environmental Protection Agency, Corvallis, Oregon; Barry Spicer, Data Branch Supervisor with the Arizona Game and Fish Department, Phoenix; M. D. F. Udvardy, California State University, Sacramento; Jan W. van Wagtendonk, Research Scientist with the National Park Service, Yosemite National Park, California, and Denis White, Oregon State University, Corvallis, for their editorial comments and review. Their helpful suggestions were as essential as they were thought-provoking and improved the manuscript immensely.

Also helpful in providing photographs and information, and otherwise assisting in this project, were Randy Babb, Arizona Game and Fish Department, Phoenix; Burt Bartram, Arizona State University, Tempe; Richard E. Brown of Meadow Vista, California; Javier Diáz of Escarcega, Campeche, Mexico; Barb Dillon, R. E. Hamburg, and Peter Neubauer, Northwest Territories Economic Development and Tourism, Canada; Nancy Gray, Great Smoky Mountains National Park, Gatlinburg, Tennessee; Jeff Grathwohl, University of Utah Press, Salt Lake City; Orie Laucks, Miami University, Oxford, Ohio; Bob Lofgren, Laboratory of Tree Ring Research, University of Arizona, Tucson; Melvin Marcus, Arizona State University, Tempe (now deceased); Paul S. Martin, Department of Geosciences, University of Arizona, Tempe; Joe McAuliffe, Thom Hulen, Ted Anderson, and Patrick Quirk of the Phoenix Desert Botanical Gardens, Arizona; Roscoe Nichols, Jr., of Ciudad Manté, Tamaulipas, Mexico; David Pearson, Arizona State University, Tempe; Bob Pfister, Montana Forest and Conservation Experiment Station, Missoula; Donald Pinkava, Arizona State University, Tempe; Bonnie Swarbrick, International Wildlife Museum, Tucson, Arizona; Raymond M. Turner, University of Arizona, Tucson; and Alejandro Velézquez, Universidad Nacional Autonoma de Mexico.

We are especially grateful to Bob Puterski, Las Vegas, Nevada, for preparing the 1:10,000,000 color map, to Peter Banka, Monmouth, Oregon, for preparing the figures, and to Gail Corbin, Las Vegas, Nevada, for word processing earlier versions of this manuscript. Their enthusiasm for this project was as valuable as their experience and is much appreciated.

Notice The U.S. Environmental Protection Agency (EPA), through its Office of Research and Development (ORD), collaborated in the research described here. This manuscript has been peer reviewed by EPA and approved for publication. Mention of trade names does not constitute endorsement or recommendation for use.

Introduction

Biotic communities are regional plant formations characterized by particular species of plants and animals. Using previous works and modifying the existing terminology of biologists, ecologists, and biogeographers, we have incorporated these biotic communities in a hierarchical classification system. This classification system is formulated on the limiting effects of moisture and temperature minima on the structure and composition of vegetation as well as specific plant and animal adaptations to regional environments, and it is used by the Rangelands Group of the Environmental Protection Agency's Environmental Monitoring and Assessment Program, the Arizona and New Mexico game and fish departments, and other Southwest agencies.

To illustrate the applicability of the classification system, the Environmental Protection Agency funded the preparation of a 1:10,000,000 map depicting the major upland biotic communities of North America using an ecological color scheme that shows gradients in moisture and temperature. Digitized and computer-compatible, this system assists biotic inventory and assessment, the delineation and stratification of habitats, and the identification of natural areas. Moreover, the biogeographical validity of the hierarchy's various categories is statistically testable through the use of existing climatic data and an analysis of plant and animal distributions. Both the classification system and map are therefore useful to anyone interested in biotic diversity.

Numerous classification systems have been created to depict and assess natural resources. In North America,* these efforts have resulted in classifications and maps of potential natural vegetation (e.g., Shantz and Zön 1924; Küchler 1964, 1977; Flores Mata et al. 1971; Rzedowski 1978; Chapman 1993), forest-types (Society of American Foresters 1954; Braun 1950; Rowe 1972), life zones (Merriam et al. 1910; Holdridge 1959, 1969), wetlands (Ray 1975; Zoltai et al. 1975; Cowardin et al. 1979; Hayden, Ray, and Dolan 1984), soils and landforms (USDA Soil Conservation Service 1975), land-

---

*We follow the definition as presented in *The American Heritage Dictionary of the English Language*, William Morris, ed., Houghton Mifflin Co. (1981):

North America—The northern continent of the Western Hemisphere with a total area, including adjacent islands, of 9,385,000 square miles. It extends from the Colombia-Panama border in the south through Central America, the United States (except Hawaii), Canada, and the Arctic Archipelago to the northern tip of Greenland.

The map, however, includes only North America, north of the Panama Canal.

use (Anderson, Hardy, and Roach 1972; Anderson et al. 1976), "ecosystems" (Crowley 1967; Meidinger and Pojar 1991), "ecoregions" (Bailey 1976; Bailey and Cushwa 1981;Wiken 1986; Wiken, Rubec, and Ironside 1989; Omernik 1987; Ricketts et al. 1997), land-cover (Loveland et al. 1991), and vegetation change (Eidenshink 1992). These resources have proven useful to those interested in land-use planning and the sampling and stratification of large-scale units, including states (see, e.g., Frye, Brown, and McMahan 1984), provinces (Wickware and Rubec 1989; MacKinnon, Meidinger, and Klinka 1992), regions (Brown and Lowe 1980, 1994), nations (Tosi 1969; Carnahan 1976; Garrison et al. 1977; Driscoll et al. 1984; Wiken, Rubec, and Ironside 1989; Borhidi 1991), and even continents (Bailey 1989a, 1989b). Although most of these classifications are based on vegetation, others incorporate physiographic, climatic, soil, geographic, and chemical criteria. Some of these classifications are hierarchical (e.g., Avers et al. 1993), thus aiding land-use mapping at various scales. Several recent maps also have the advantage of being derived from high-altitude imagery and are thus applicable for the demonstration and assessment of vegetative and other changes over time (e.g., Loveland et al. 1991; Stacey and Knighton 1994). The only criticism of these classifications and maps is that their usefulness is necessarily limited by the methodology employed and the designing organization's mission, objectives, and budget.

None of the above classifications, however, has been universally adopted by biologists in their efforts to classify and inventory plant and animal habitats. Systems and maps currently used by biologists either are based on existing vegetation without regard to regional plant and animal associates, or rely upon one or more land-use classifications that employ anthropogenic and other "nonbiocentric" criteria. Many of the classifications presently in use (e.g., Küchler 1964) are nonhierarchical or only partially hierarchical. As such, these systems and maps are frequently limited and are not easily modified when higher or lower levels of assessment are desired. These limitations have caused resource management agencies to combine, create, and adapt a variety of classification systems in their inventories of biotic resources. The result has been a proliferation of large and small scale maps, either depicting only limited areas (e.g., Brown and Lowe 1980, 1994), or employing classifications that are too broad for detailed biological enquiry (e.g., Bailey and Cushwa 1981).

The profusion of classification systems has prompted national governments to seek a singular, standardized system. Canada has adopted an "official" national resource classification system (see, e.g., Wiken 1986, Meidinger and Pojar 1991, and MacKinnon, Meidinger, and Klinka 1992). Uniform vegetation classification systems have recently been proposed for Europe (Neuhäusl 1990) and for certain United States government agencies (Nature Conservancy 1994a, 1994b). Recently, a standardized vegetation classification system has been developed for use by all federal government agencies in the United States (U.S. Department of Interior Federal Geographic Data Committee 1995). These efforts, coupled with the accelerated inventory of the world's biota and the development of high quality aerial imagery, now make biologically universal classification systems and maps possible both theoretically and practically.

The need for a federal standardized method of inventorying both plant and animal habitats is obvious, given the requirements of the National Environmental Policy Act of 1969, the National Resource Planning Act of 1974, and the U.S. Environmental Protection Agency's Environmental Monitoring and Assessment Program. Such a classification system, however, should not be confined to the United States and its territories. The present and increasing emphasis on endangered species residing within and outside the United States embodied in the Endangered Species Act of 1973, the North American Waterfowl Plan, the Neotropical Migratory Bird inventories now being supervised by the U.S. Fish and Wildlife Service, and the Biosphere Reserve Program being fostered by the Union for the Conservation of Nature dictate a worldwide approach to biotic assessment. While national vegetation classification systems are highly desirable for administrative purposes, these systems must also be compatible with the needs of scholars, and of those zoologists and biologists who work with international agencies.

1

The
Biogeographic
Approach

Humans have long been aware that certain plants and animals were found in different areas and at different altitudes. It was not until the middle of the eighteenth century, however, that naturalists began formulating hypotheses to explain the differences and similarities they had observed. Carl Linnaeus commented on the dependence of vegetation on soil, climate, and elevation, and the French naturalist Georges Buffon postulated the effects of elevation and geographic barriers on plant and animal distribution (see Kendeigh 1952, Udvardy 1969, and Sterling 1974 for detailed summaries of the early history of the biogeographic concept). Then, in the early 1800s, Alexander von Humboldt and his botanist accomplice Aime Bonpland wrote a series of essays laying the theoretical foundation for understanding the distribution of plants. In such works as their *Geography of Plants* (Humboldt and Bonpland 1807) and Humboldt's *The Geographic Distribution of Plants* (1817), they described the effects of temperature on corresponding latitudinal and altitudinal belts of vegetation in the South American Andes. Humboldt also realized that animal distributions followed similar "rules," and he is rightfully regarded as the "father of biogeography."

A generation later, the great naturalist Louis Agassiz (1854) divided the world into eight continental land masses or "realms" based on their faunal constituents and the human races living there. This largely intuitive effort was followed by British ornithologist Phillip Lutley Sclater (1858), who presented a similar division of the world based on the then known distribution of birds. Although Sclater's six faunal "regions" bore a strong similarity to Agassiz's "realms," his classification was based on a sounder theoretical basis, and his concept received wide recognition. Accordingly, Sclater's work was soon being modified and rearranged by zoologists in other fields, including other ornithologists such as Thomas Huxley (1868).

Using Sclater's model, and incorporating his and Charles Darwin's theories on evolution, as well as his considerable experience with the biota of both hemispheres, A. R. Wallace (1876) published a rationale and map dividing the world into six biogeographic "regions" based on the distribution of mammalian orders and families. Although Wallace's six regions were similar to Sclater's, Wallace went a step further and subdivided his regions into twenty-four "subregions" or "provinces" based on the then-known distribution of mammal genera and species. His Nearctic Region of North America, for example, contained a Canadian, an Eastern United States, a

Rocky Mountain, and a California province. Recognizing the importance of geographic origin and isolation as well as of climate, his
Geographical Distribution of Animals soon became accepted as the
standard approach to biogeography.

Wallace's ideas did not go unchallenged. J. A. Allen, a contempo-
rary American mammalogist, took strong issue with the delineations
of Wallace's regions. Allen (1878, 1892) proposed instead a system
of eight "realms" or "faunal areas," which, while equivalent to Wallace's regions, contained in descending rank "regions," "provinces,"
and, lastly, a series of "floras and faunas." Although insightful and
ahead of his time (Allen recognized a circumpolar Arctic Realm, and
combined Wallace's Nearctic and Palearctic regions into a "Holarctic" or North Temperate Realm), Allen's approach was less analytical
than Wallace's. Partly for this reason, Allen's biogeographic classification and its hierarchy were rejected in favor of the Sclater-Wallace
approach.

Later, another American zoologist, Theodore Gill (1885), compared Wallace's and Allen's systems. While generally favoring the
former, Gill had a number of pertinent criticisms of both approaches.
In a well-considered but now largely forgotten paper, Gill followed
his predecessors' approach in dividing the world's continental land
masses into large "faunal realms" on the basis of animal orders and
families. As had Wallace and Allen, he used genera to delineate a hierarchy of finer "regions" and other subdivisions. Gill objected,
however, to the use by Wallace and Allen of only mammals as the
defining criteria in their classifications. Gill, an ichthyologist,
thought that all animals should be used, including fishes. Like Wallace, Gill recognized that isolation and evolution were equally as important as temperature in determining terrestrial realms. He also
noted the lack of marine forms in previous classifications—an omission only now being readdressed (see, e.g., Ray 1975, Maxwell et al.
1994). To correct this omission, Gill proposed the addition of six
marine realms determined primarily on water temperatures—an
Arctic Realm, a Paractalian or North Temperate Realm, a Tropical
Realm, a Notalian or South Temperate Realm, an Antarctican
Realm, and a Deep Sea or Bassalian Realm.

Botanists meanwhile were hard at work developing their own
phytogeographic classifications. As early as 1859, J. G. Cooper had
divided North America into twenty-seven "natural provinces" and
regional subdivisions, giving each one a geographic or Native American name to emphasize its geographic center. Cooper also considered climate and animal constituents in his delineations, so that his
approach was biogeographic as well as vegetative. Years later, some
of his designations were still being followed by L. R. Dice (1943) and
other twentieth-century biogeographers in their efforts to identify
biotic provinces or regions.

Engler (1879–1882), a German professor of botany, was the
Wallace of plant geographers, separating the world into floral king-
doms or realms, regions, provinces, and districts analogous to Wallace's regions and provinces. Another German botany professor,

Oscar Drüde (1887) would later publish the best world vegetation map for years to come. Drüde was well aware of the limiting effects of climate on plant structure, and his map of vegetation life-forms or "formations" illustrates much more than vegetation *per se*. Besides creating and defining the formation term to designate plant structure, Drüde contributed greatly to the advancement of phytogeography through his use of hierarchy and his understanding of the effects of physiographic features on plant dispersal. As was Wallace's classification, Engler's work continued to be modified by plant and animal geographers, and, in modified form, is still used today (see, e.g., Good 1964 and Walter 1973). Although continually being revised and refined (e.g., Sclater and Sclater 1889; Udvardy 1987), the Sclater-Wallace-Engler approach has stood the test of time and remains largely intact at the continental (that is, realms or regions) level. Wallace's and Engler's provinces and other lesser ranks, never intended to be definitive or final, were in need of major revision almost immediately. Rearranging and redefining these continental subdivisions continues to occupy the attention of biogeographers to the present day.

As the nineteenth century came to a close, the United States was unique in that the federal government actively supported biogeographic inquiry. The idea for a national biological survey had originated in 1853 with Spencer Fullerton Baird of the National Museum's Smithsonian Institution. Baird saw to it that U.S. military expeditions had naturalists collecting examples of the expanding nation's flora and fauna. The results of these surveys were then published in lengthy tomes by the U.S. Congress. In 1885, after much bureaucratic wrangling, future government surveys became the responsibility of the U.S. Biological Survey, a bureau of the Department of Agriculture. The methodology to describe the habitats of the plants and animals collected on these surveys would now become, for better or worse, the domain of the Survey's first Chief, Clinton Hart Merriam.

Merriam had been taken by his well-connected father to meet Baird in 1871 (Sterling 1977). Baird was so impressed with the fifteen-year-old Merriam that he invited him to join the F. V. Hayden Survey of western Wyoming that was to be conducted by the U.S. Geological Survey the following year. While on the Hayden Survey, Merriam visited the Great Salt Lake and much of Montana, Idaho, and Wyoming, including the Grand Tetons and the newly created Yellowstone National Park. This experience so impressed him that he embarked on a lifelong career of conducting surveys and collecting specimens. Educated at Yale and well connected in the world of Washington politics (he became a personal friend of President Theodore Roosevelt), Merriam was a logical choice to head the Biological Survey, which he helped found in 1885.

Although he was later to specialize in mammals, Merriam was originally an ornithologist. An avid hunter and collector, Merriam maintained a strong interest in the geographic distribution of animals all his life. Experienced, fastidious, and a tireless worker, Merriam

appeared to be eminently suited for his role as America's chief bio-
geographer. He was also productive, authoring the first eleven of the
Survey's North American Fauna series that he initiated in 1889 and
that continued until 1959 (Murie 1959). Most importantly, he recognized, to his everlasting credit, that biogeographical understanding
could not be limited by political boundaries. Accordingly, he saw to
it that his agency conducted biological investigations throughout the
North American continent from the Canadian Arctic to the tropical
regions of Central America (see, e.g., Merriam 1903, Stejneger and
Miller 1903, and Goldman 1920).

In 1889 Merriam took time off from his duties in Washington to
conduct a biological survey of the San Francisco Peaks and its envi-
rons in northern Arizona Territory. While conducting this investigation, Merriam and his partner Leonhard Stejneger noted, as did
Humboldt, that the altitudinal belts of vegetation encountered at different elevations corresponded to the vegetation found at various lat-
itudes. What was more, the animals they collected in these "life
zones," as Merriam called them, were also similar to their latitudinal
counterparts. Carefully measuring their altitudes, Merriam postulated that the single most important factor determining life zones was
temperature. Based on actual observations and the collection of
"indicator species" of plants and animals, Merriam and Stejneger's
*Results of a Biological Survey of the San Francisco Mountain Region
and Desert of the Little Colorado in Arizona* (1890) was immediately recognized as a significant contribution to the science of biogeography. Not satisfied with a regional system, Merriam (1892)
expanded their findings to prepare an advanced "life areas" map of
North America using mammalian distribution and other data.

Merriam was convinced that his life zones could be used to describe the biological affiliation of all the plants and animals in North
America. Each life zone, he concluded, was determined by temperature, with humidity, topography, and other factors being of lesser importance. To provide a scientific foundation for his life-zone theories,
Merriam conducted an *ex post facto* analysis of his distribution data
and postulated the effects of various temperature parameters. The
northward distribution of animals and plants, he reasoned, was restricted by the total quantity of heat during the growing season when
temperatures exceeded 6°C. Conversely, he concluded that the southward distribution of species was determined by the mean temperatures experienced during the hottest six weeks of the year. Using
tables of summed temperature data provided by the U.S. Weather
Bureau, Merriam and his colleagues in the Survey proceeded to publish a series of articles and maps showing regional and continental
life zones (see, e.g., Merriam 1894a, 1894b, 1898, and Merriam et
al. 1910). The biogeographic affiliation problem was declared
solved. From now on the work of the Survey would be much simpli-
fied and its collected specimens could be pigeonholed in their proper
life zone categories.

Merriam's exalted position firmly established the life-zone concept as the official biogeographic classification system for the U.S.

Biological Survey. Other mammalogists and ornithologists, especially in the West (e.g., Hall, Monroe, and Grinnell 1919; Hall 1946), also became strong life-zone supporters in that life zones were based on actual altitudinal gradients that could be recognized on the basis of indicator species. Even though Merriam's climatic calculations did not consider humidity, aridity, or minimum temperatures, criticism from biologists was slow in coming. Also ignored, at least for the time being, was his failure to adequately consider such factors as regional isolation.

Few botanists, and none of the European zoologists, adopted Merriam's life-zone classification system. Plant geographers continued instead to construct vegetation maps based on plant formations and indicator dominants (e.g., Harshberger 1911; Shreve 1917; Shantz and Zön 1924). Moreover, after Merriam's departure from the Survey in 1910, biologists in other institutions began to take issue with his maps and temperature data (e.g., Livingston and Shreve 1921). Not only were Merriam's temperature summations faulty and shown to be almost meaningless as limiting factors, his maps and terminology were found to have little application in the Eastern United States or the tropics (Dice 1923; Kendeigh 1932; Shelford 1932a, 1945; Daubenmire 1938, 1946). After nearly fifty years of controversy, Merriam's life-zone system, initially a sound biogeographic study of a Western mountain, was repudiated on the basis of faulty premises, incorrect data, and the fact that it just did not work outside of the American West, where it remains in limited use today.

Botanists in the meantime were doing better with their vegetation hierarchies, dividing the world into climatic zones, formation classes, communities, and associations (see, e.g., Clements 1916, Braun-Blanquet 1932, Weaver and Clements 1938, and Küchler 1947). After 1900, plant ecologists approached vegetation classification from several viewpoints (Whittaker 1978; McIntosh 1985). Following the European tradition set by Drüde (1887) and Warming (1909), H. C. Cowles (1908), Frederick E. Clements (1916), and other ecologists set about classifying vegetation in the United States, as did A. G. Tansley (1923) in Great Britain. Most of these ecologists took "a top-down" or landscape physiognomy approach that classified plant communities on the basis of dominance-types (Whittaker 1978). Emphasizing structural dominants as "indicator species," Clements (1920) was especially influential in America, and his concept of the plant community as a holistic organism, which, with the cessation of disruptive influences, would progress toward a self-sustaining climax controlled by climate and edaphic (soil) conditions, was widely accepted.

Another school of thought took a more formal "bottom-up" or floristic approach. Chief among these was the Braun-Blanquet (1932) system, which is widely used in both Europe and America. In this system, vegetation samples or *relevés* are grouped into units on the basis of the similarity of the composition of character (that is, indicator) species. The basic unit in this classification is the "association." Each association is then grouped into higher units called alliances. Alliances are, in turn, grouped into orders, and orders into classes, to produce a formal hierarchy of community classification. Even the higher units are based on floristic relationships rather than physiognomy (Whittaker 1962; Mueller-Dombois and Ellenberg 1974). The difference between these two schools is then one of landscapes vs. floristics.

At the same time that Clements was espousing his plant community theories, H. A. Gleason (1926) was stressing that, rather than a plant community evolving as a whole, plants and plant species adapted individually to climatic parameters within the community or association. Forrest Shreve (1951) also objected to some of Clements's concepts regarding succession. Shreve had noted that succession in the Clementian sense did not take place in desert environments, and he used the term "prevailing vegetation" rather than "climax" when describing landscapes. Later studies and evidence have tended to support both Gleason's and Shreve's views regarding these aspects (Whittaker 1978; Holling 1995; Graham et al. 1996). Similarly, Weaver and Clements's (1938) ideas on plant succession and climax, while earning widespread recognition (and criticism), have proven too local and unpredictable for general use.

Both the physionomic and floristic approaches have strengths and weaknesses. Various regional traditions and modifications also have served to improve the vegetation classification processes of both schools (see, e.g., U.S. Department of Interior FGDC 1995, and Nature Conservancy 1997), and both schools have their adherents and their detractors, who have developed a confusing array of terminology in their efforts to describe the various units of their classifications. Nonetheless, no one system is necessarily "the best" system for all aspects of ecological inventory.

Observing that vegetation samples taken by unprejudiced means yielded a large proportion of mixed, atypical, and transitional associations, Whittaker (1962) concluded that many plant species grade into other types of vegetation, and that there was a lack of "discontinuity" between communities. This "continuum" within and between communities has prompted some botanists to question whether vegetation should be classified at all. Whittaker (1962:159) thought that vegetation classification might be more art than science, and that future efforts to improve classification should be directed less toward standardization and a quest for objectivity, than toward a more realistic understanding of the process of classification and its relation to the properties of the communities involved.

Using various classifications, phytogeographers have mapped the potential (that is, prevailing) natural vegetation of nations (e.g., Küchler 1964 for the United States; Rzedowski 1978 for Mexico; and Borhidi 1991 for Cuba). Plant communities have been the basis for many state and regional maps (see, e.g., Wieslander 1935, Jensen 1947, Miller 1951, Barbour and Major 1977, and Küchler 1977 for California). An especially innovative system based on climatic and structural criteria was devised in tropical America by Holdridge

(1967). Complex, and difficult to apply without a myriad of climatological stations, Holdridge's classification system is nonetheless based on a strong theoretical foundation. Although Holdridge's formulae are not applicable to temperate America (see, e.g., MacMahon and Wieboldt 1983), his system has been used in modified form to map vegetation in Central America (e.g., Tosi 1969; Jennings 1988). Another, more "European," vegetation classification system has recently been used to successfully describe and map Cuba's natural vegetation (Borhidi 1991). Several of these recent vegetation classification systems incorporate evolutionary-based levels in their hierarchies (e.g., Takhtajan's [1986] floristic regions). For these reasons, vegetation classifications and maps are the foundation of most habitat descriptions (e.g., Carr 1950; Leopold 1959; Robbins, Bruun, and Zim 1966).

Plant communities, however, do not necessarily correspond to animal habitats because of different evolutionary and dispersal histories (see, e.g., Dice 1923). Many plant community classifications (e.g., Braun-Blanquet 1932; Holdridge 1967; Mueller-Dombois and Ellenberg 1974) are too structurally detailed to be adopted by zoogeographers. It is also true that even when vegetation classification systems take ecological limitations such as climate into account, they often fail to consider regional isolation and other evolutionary forces (see, e.g., Wieslander 1935, Jensen 1947, and Küchler 1964, 1977). Nonetheless, the merging of the two disciplines—the geographic grouping of animal habitats paralleling vegetation classification systems—continues to be a useful tool for many biologists (Udvardy 1969; Maycock 1979).

Recognizing the importance of plant habitats on animal distributions, zoogeographers began to use plant assemblages to elaborate on Wallace's and Gill's faunal subdivisions. Based on the number and presence of animal species and subspecies, these subdivisions became known as biotic provinces in North America and biogeographical provinces in Europe (Vestal 1914; Gleason 1926; Dice 1943; Goldman and Moore 1945; Matvejev 1961; McLachlan and Liversidge 1962; Udvardy 1969, 1975a, 1975b, 1984a, 1984b). Generally speaking, biotic provinces are determined on the basis of regional climate, topography and soils, and a similarity in plant and animal constituents. As such, biotic provinces are regional faunal and plant assemblages that share a common geologic and evolutionary history (Miller 1951; Kendeigh 1952). In essence, Merriam's 1890 life zone map of the San Francisco Peaks was a biotic province map (Daubenmire 1938). Some biologists, (e.g., Dice 1943) also considered biotic provinces as centers for ecological dispersal.

The biotic equivalent of a plant formation, in a concept conceived by Clements and Shelford (1939), was the biome. Modifying earlier vegetation maps, Clements and Shelford mapped eleven biomes in North America to show the applicability of such an approach. They were not disappointed. Biologists such as Pitelka (1941), Miller (1951), and Aldrich (1967) readily adopted and adapted the biome concept in their studies, some of them substituting the term "biotic community" for biome. Although Shelford (1963) considered the biotic community designation redundant, he had used it himself (Shelford 1932b), and the two terms have become almost synonymous.

Nonetheless, biomes, as originally defined, did not include regional descriptions reflecting evolutionary and climatic influences, and many applications of the biome term were finer subdivisions than was originally intended. In an effort to clarify biotic terminology, Kendeigh (1952) defined a biotic community as a biociation, each biociation having a distinctive species composition and occurring in a particular vegetation type that had become differentiated due to isolation and evolution. These biotic communities (or biociations) were in turn composed of one or more plant associations. Kendeigh also proposed that the name of each biotic community contain the type of vegetation involved, and that when it was necessary to distinguish one biotic community from another having the same type of vegetation, a geographical name also be used—e.g., California chaparral. This description fits the general understanding of a biotic community presented here.

As have their plant ecologist counterparts, zoologists have come to accept Gleason's (1926) concept that individual members of a community can, and do, evolve independently of the biotic community in which they reside. Clements's (1920) view of the community as a holistic superorganism composed of a highly ordered sequence of species maturing toward a sustainable climax whose characteristics are determined by climate and soil conditions has accordingly been greatly revised (see, e.g., Whittaker 1978 and Holling 1995). We no longer think of climax communities as evolving superorganisms, and instead recognize the temporal and spatial nature of plant and animal community hierarchy. Clements was a great ecologist, nonetheless, and many of his contributions remain valid in modified form. He was one of the first to note that plant and animal communities change and move with climatic shifts, and many of his ecological terms such as "disclimax" (permanently altered), "post-climax" (overmature), and "consociation" (single species dominant) remain useful landscape descriptions. Plant and animal communities remain, despite the limitations of Clements and Shelford's (1939) original concepts, a system of interacting populations having a particular structure and function (Whittaker 1962). Thus, the biotic approach is the best available tool in our efforts to describe plant and animal habitats.

The advantages of a biotic-community approach over purely vegetative classification systems have been pointed out by a number of biologists, including Shelford (1945), Odum (1945), Kendeigh (1952), Udvardy (1969), and Brown, Lowe, and Pase (1980). In summary, these include, but are not limited to, the following:

    1. Biotic communities recognize faunal as well as floral distributions, thereby allowing inferences to be made as to the occurrence and relative abundance of specific plants and animals

within a given formation-type. The biotic-community designation thus facilitates the meaningful inventory of common species as well as rare and endangered ones. For example, most populations of the eastern fox squirrel (*Sciurus niger*), as well as the rare and endangered red-cockaded woodpecker (*Dendrocopos borealis*) are contained within the Southeastern Deciduous and Evergreen Forest biotic community.

2. Biotic communities are readily recognized in the field, and their boundaries can be mapped on the basis of a formation-type's principal plant dominants and the species of plants and animals known to be present therein (i.e., indicator species).

3. In conjunction with biotic provinces, biotic communities and their subdivisions provide a hierarchical measurement of the length of time of ecological isolation within the continental or realm level. Even when exotic plants and animals invade "native communities" to the extent of achieving ecological dominance, a total replacement of the native biota is rare, and the biotic affiliation of these now "disclimax" or "new-alien" communities can usually be readily ascertained and incorporated into the classification system.

4. Biotic communities, by their very nature, express the effects of all interacting environmental factors, abiotic as well as biotic, thus simplifying the classification of plant and animal communities. Although soil properties and landform history affect water storage, and therefore determine the composition of plant communities within biotic provinces (see, e.g., Dokuchaev 1987 and McAuliffe 1995), our understanding of soil types is insufficient to predict which biotic community will be present on a given soil type (edaphic climax). And, even though certain plant communities, and even local plant formations, may be restricted to serpentines, gypsum, or other special soil types, the complexity involved precludes using soil type and other abiotic factors to construct a biotic classification system. Rather, it appears more reasonable to let the biotic components of a community indicate which soil types are likely to be present.

5. Although biotic communities are initially identified and delineated on the basis of plant dominants, an increasing body of data on indicator species now permits the relative ranking of various biotic communities by comparing the percentages of common plants and animals present (or absent) at the genus, species, and subspecies levels. Furthermore, the "reality" of biotic communities can be statistically evaluated by testing differences in seasonal climatic data, degrees of endemism, and similarities and differences in species composition (see, e.g., Pearson and Cassola 1992 and Pearson 1994).

6. The biotic community designation is flexible; units may be added, combined, or deleted as research and analysis warrants. Moreover, the inclusion of biotic communities in a classification system incorporates more than a century of effort in the development of zoogeographic and phytogeographic systematics.

Although no habitat classification system based on a biogeographic hierarchy and using biotic community concepts has yet received universal acceptance, systems based on such an integrated approach are becoming increasingly common (e.g., Driscoll et al. 1984; Pojar, Klinka, and Meidinger 1987; Bailey 1989a, 1989b; Neuhäusl 1990; Meidinger and Pojar 1991; Avers et al. 1993; Demarchi 1993). Even among those biologists who consider the concept of biotic communities as an "obsolete science," in that it is no longer believed that plant and animal dominants form discrete communities, these basic descriptions remain the backbone of discussions pertaining to plant-animal habitat relationships. Ecologists who view communities as a non-discrete and dynamic continuum find that they cannot resist the logic, convenience, and descriptive value of geographically and ecologically pigeonholing the various assemblages of plants and animals living within certain physical conditions and parameters. This acceptance is encouraging in that biologists have long utilized and benefited from the analogous perceived order of hierarchical systematics in plants and animals (Linnaeus 1758, Simpson 1961).

2

The
Classification
System

"On two main points every system yet proposed, or that probably can be proposed, is open to objection; they are,— 1stly, that the several regions are not of equal rank; 2ndly, that they are not equally applicable to all classes . . ."
—Alfred Russel Wallace, 1876

Modifying the existing works and terminology of other biologists, ecologists, and biogeographers, Brown, Lowe, and Pase (1979, 1980) developed a hierarchical classification system for the biotic communities of North America. This classification system depends on natural criteria and recognizes the limiting effects of moisture and temperature minima as well as evolutionary origin on the structure and composition of plant and animal communities. The system was originally developed for southwestern North America where its adaptability was demonstrated for both natural and human-altered communities (Brown and Lowe 1974a, 1974b, 1980, 1994; Brown 1980, 1982). Because the classification system is both parallel and hierarchical (fig. 1), it is adaptable for use at various levels of detail. Mapping can be at any scale or unit of resolution. Moreover, the hierarchical sequence allows for the incorporation of existing vegetation classification taxa in use by federal, state, and private agencies into an appropriate biotic community level within the classification system (see, e.g., Nature Conservancy 1994a, 1994b, and Bourgeron et al. 1995).

The numerical coding of the hierarchy also makes the classification system computer compatible, thereby readily allowing for the storage and retrieval of information. The Brown, Lowe, and Pase (1979, 1980) system for the North American Southwest is currently in use in the RUN WILD program developed for use on remote terminals by the USDA Forest Service's Southwestern Region and Rocky Mountain Forest and Range Experiment Station (Patton 1978). This classification system is similarly incorporated within the files of the Arizona and New Mexico game and fish departments, and is used in environmental analysis procedures as required by the National Environmental Policy Act (e.g., Reichenbacher 1990). It was adopted by the Arid Ecosystems Resource Group of the U.S. Environmental Protection Agency for their Environmental Monitoring and Assessment Program (EMAP).

This classification system facilitates biotic inventory and assessment, the delineation and stratification of habitats, resource

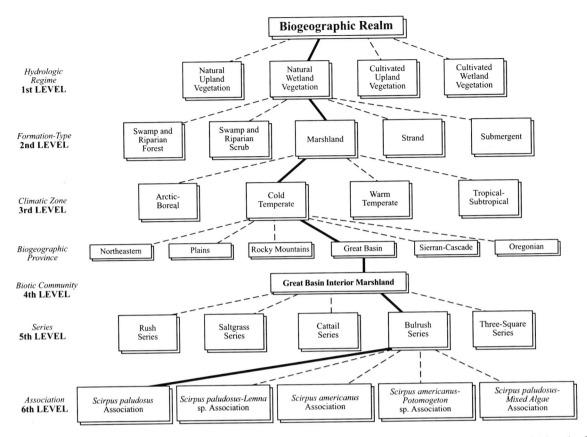

Figure 1. Heirarchy of a bulrush marsh in Great Salt Lake, Utah, to the association (sixth) level of the classification system.

planning, the interpretation of biological values, and other activities pertaining to natural history inquiry. It has proven especially useful for environmental analysis where the comparison of biological units is desired by governmental, scientific, educational, and other institutions. In short, the classification system is of particular use for those interested in inventorying biotic diversity for resource management, vegetation change, biological study, natural area preservation, and habitat acquisition. Moreover, because the system is hierarchical and universal, earlier inventory efforts can almost always be accommodated into it at some level.

The ultimate value of any environmental classification system is the meaningful assignment of plant and animal habitats. Although most of the system's hierarchies are identified on the basis of observable vegetation, the inclusion of biogeographic realm, biotic province, and biotic community criteria automatically incorporates the less visible animal components into the classification. The system therefore allows for a more meaningful delineation and inventory of specific plant and animal habitats. For example, because biotic-province criteria are included in the system, a resource manager can determine which marshlands are likely to include nesting black ducks (*Anas rubripes*) as opposed to similar-structured wetlands within other biotic provinces inhabited by Florida ducks (*A. fulvigula ful-*

vigula), mottled ducks *(A. f. maculosa),* and Mexican ducks *(A. platyrhynchos diazi).* Such separations of plant and animal habitats are important in fulfilling the requirements of the Endangered Species Act, for evaluating the North American Waterfowl Plan, for monitoring warblers and other migratory birds of recent concern, and for following numerous other governmental directives. The inclusion of biogeographic criteria is also of primary importance in the world biosphere reserve program (see, e.g., Franklin 1977, McNeely and Miller 1983, Udvardy 1984a, 1984b, and IUCN 1974).

The hierarchy is not rigorously systematic. Some of the equivalents at certain levels are greater in extent, and therefore importance, than others (e.g., at the fourth or biotic community level the Northeastern Deciduous Forest is much larger in area and far greater in importance than Rocky Mountain Alpine Tundra). But such anomalies are common in biological systematics; the variety and distribution of the Passeriformes are greater than in the Gaviiformes, even though both orders have equal rank within the class Aves.

Although the hierarchy reflects scales, it is not scale dependent. For example, a 10-m^2 area of grass could be an interspace within Great Basin Conifer Woodland if the objective is a biotic community map at a scale of 1:125,000. This same area could also be Intermountain Grassland if one were sampling an association to be mapped at a scale of 1:15,625.

Our purpose in presenting this classification system is neither to promote a new concept nor to replace existing classifications. Instead, we are attempting to present a hierarchical synthesis of the existing works on North American biogeography to aid in the development of a universal classification system for the world's natural environments. We recognize that portions of the classification system are dated or incomplete and require additional work. For example, climatic data are now available from a great variety of stations, and we are currently refining the temperature parameters of the climatic zones to make them more precise and meaningful. Also, the integrities of the various biotic community levels of the classification are presently testable through scientific methodologies, and we are now evaluating the "reality" of several biotic communities through a statistical analysis of seasonal climatological data. This analysis, and the recent acceleration in floristic and faunistic inventories, will help determine the reality of these and possibly other biotic communities.

Presented below is a computer-compatible hierarchy of the world's biological systems with representative examples of the classification to the series (5th) level for North America. Neither the biotic community (4th) level, nor the series level examples of the classification are complete or final. Examples of the association (6th) level of the system are given only for the Rocky Mountain Montane Conifer Forest biotic community. Unlike previous presentations of the classification system (Brown and Lowe 1974a, 1974b; Brown, Lowe, and Pase 1979, 1980; Brown 1980), in which North America's biotic communities were all contained within the Nearctic biogeographical realm, the classification presented here properly separates the

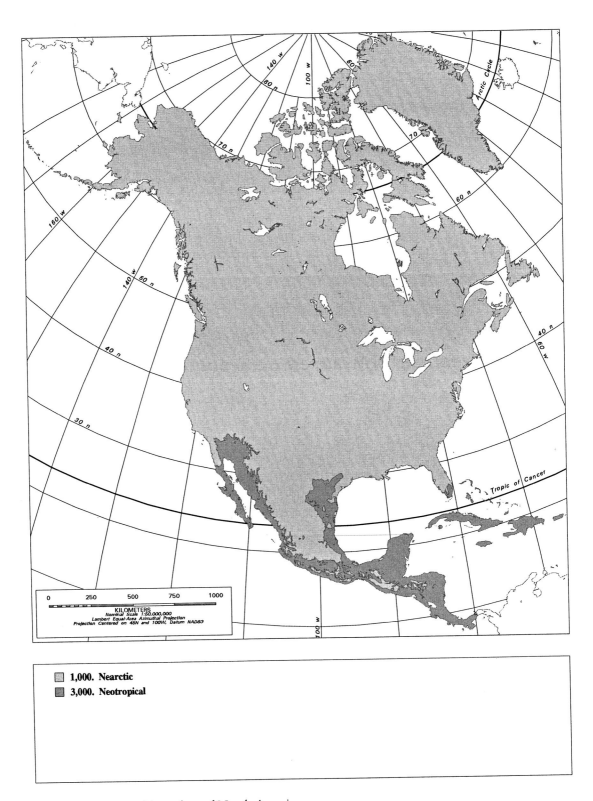

1,000. Nearctic
3,000. Neotropical

Figure 2. Biogeographic realms of North America.

continent into Nearctic and Neotropical realms (fig. 2). Remote off-shore islands such as Mexico's Revilla Gigedo islands are considered as possessing distinctive biotic communities within an Oceanic realm.

A description of each level of the classification system follows the outline below, where

    1,000 = Biogeographic Realm
      1,100 = Hydrologic Regime
        1,110 = Formation-type
          1,111 = Climatic Zone
            1,111.1 = Biotic Community (Regional Formation)
              1,111.11 = Series
                          (Alliance of Generic Dominants)
                1,111.111 = Association
                            (Plant community of specific taxa)
                  1,111.1111 = Plant and Animal Density,
                              Plant Age Class, etc.

The number preceding the comma (e.g., 1,000) differentiates the hierarchy on the basis of the world's biogeographic realms (table 1). Origin and evolutionary history are thus recognized as being of primary importance in the determination and classification of biotic entities. The mappable reality of the world's biogeographical realms is, as in all natural taxonomy, interpretive and dependent on the criteria used. The following seven realms are adapted from Sclater (1858), Wallace (1876), Allen (1892, 1893), Sharpe (1893), Hesse, Allee, and Schmidt (1937), Darlington (1957), Dansereau (1957), Walter (1973), the International Union for Conservation of Nature and Natural Resources (IUCN 1974), DeLaubenfels (1975), Cox, Healey, and Moore (1976), and Udvardy (1975a, 1975b, 1984a).

1,000 Nearctic—Continental North America exclusive of the tropics including most of the highland areas of Mexico and northern Central America (fig. 2).

2,000 Palearctic—Eurasia exclusive of the tropics; Africa north of the Sahel.

3,000 Neotropical and Antarctican—South America, most of Mexico and Central America below an altitude of ca. 1,000 meters, southern Florida, extreme southern Texas, and the Sonoran Desert region of California and Arizona (fig. 2). Also included here are New Zealand, the Falkland (Maldive) Islands, and other southern islands having an Arctic-Boreal (Antarctic-Austral) climatic regime and designated as belonging to the Antarctic Realm of Udvardy (1975a, 1987).

4,000 Indomalayan (Oriental)—Southeast Asia, the Indian subcontinent, Indonesia, the Philippines, etc.

5,000 African (Afrotropical)—Africa south of the Sahara, and the southern portion of the Arabian peninsula.

6,000 Australian—Australia and Tasmania.

7,000 Oceanic—Oceanic islands displaying a high degree of endemism, for example, the Hawaiian Islands, Madagascar, and New Guinea. Although the Oceanic or Oceanian realm designation usually refers to the islands of the South Pacific (Udvardy 1996, un-publ. ms.), the term is used here more as a "catch-all" realm in that each pelagic island, or island group, has a distinctive evolutionary history that is more or less independent of continental influences.

The assignation of the boundary between North America's Nearctic and Neotropical realms is not clear-cut and is, therefore, arbitrary in part. Even though the fauna of the Sonoran, Tamaulipan, and Floridian biotic provinces contains both Nearctic and Neotropical animals, the flora of these provinces is largely Neotropical. We have, therefore, included Sonoran Desertscrub, Tamaulipan Thornscrub, and Floridian Evergreen Forest in the Neotropical Realm. Conversely, biotic communities such as Veracruz and Guatemalan cloud forests, which possess a largely Nearctic flora, but an almost entirely Neotropical fauna, are here contained within the Nearctic Realm. Florida's "Everglades," possessing both a Nearctic and a Neotropical biota, but isolated by the waters surrounding the Florida peninsula, is classified tentatively here as a Nearctic Wetland.

First Level   The first digit *after* the comma (e.g., 1,<u>1</u>00) refers to one of four **hydrologic regimes** that include all upland (1,100) and wetland (1,200) communities existing under natural conditions. The important adaptations of plants and animals to terrestrial ecosystems, as opposed to wetland systems, are thus recognized early in the classification system. The classification of aquatic or submerged freshwater (e.g., 1,300) and marine (e.g., 1,400) environments is as yet in a tentative stage (see, e.g., Maxwell et al. 1994). Although accommodated in the system, the classification of these "open-water" communities is outside the scope of this work and is not included here. Also not included here, but included within the system, are terrestrial and wetland croplands and other human-maintained environments (Brown 1980). Because almost all "natural communities" are now more or less influenced by human activity, we include all native, naturalized, and adventive plant communities as belonging to either a natural upland or a natural wetland regime even though the vegetation may be in a successional, a man-altered, or even a disclimax condition (table 1).

In this classification system, wetlands include all periodically, seasonally, or continually submerged lands populated by emergent plants and life-forms different from the immediately adjacent upland vegetation (see also, e.g., Martin et al. 1953, Lowe 1964, and Cowardin et al. 1979). Hence, riparian communities containing both upland and wetland components are included here in the natural wetland regime (e.g., 1,200, table 1).

Second Level   The second digit after the comma, (e.g., 1,1<u>1</u>0) refers to one of the following recognized plant formations, or, as they are called on a worldwide basis, **formation-types** (table 2, fig. 3). Formation-types are vegetative responses to integrated environmental factors, most importantly, available soil moisture.

Table 1. Summary of the world's natural vegetation to the first level

		Hydrologic Regime	
Biogeographic Realm		**Natural Upland Vegetation**	**Natural Wetland Vegetation**
1,000	Nearctic	1,100	1,200
2,000	Palearctic	2,100	2,200
3,000	Neotropical-Antarctican	3,100	3,200
4,000	Indomalayan (Oriental)	4,100	4,200
5,000	African (Afrotropical)	5,100	5,200
6,000	Australian	6,100	6,200
7,000	Oceanic	7,100	7,200

Table 2. Summary for the natural upland and wetland vegetation of the world to the second level

		Formation-type					
Biogeographic Realm		**Tundra**	**Forest and Woodland**	**Scrubland**	**Grassland**	**Desertland**	**Non-Vegetated**
UPLAND							
1,100	Nearctic	1,110	1,120	1,130	1,140	1,150	1,160
2,100	Palearctic	2,110	2,120	2,130	2,140	2,150	2,160
3,100	Neotropical-Antarctican	3,110	3,120	3,130	3,140	3,150	3,160
4,100	Indomalayan (Oriental)	4,110	4,120	4,130	4,140	4,150	4,160
5,100	African (Afrotropical)	5,110	5,120	5,130	5,140	5,150	5,160
6,100	Australian	6,110	6,120	6,130	6,140	6,150	6,160
7,100	Oceanic	7,110	7,120	7,130	7,140	7,150	7,160
		Wet Tundra	**Forest***	**Swamp Scrub**	**Marshland**	**Strand**	**Non-Vegetated**
WETLAND							
1,200	Nearctic	1,210	1,220	1,230	1,240	1,250	1,260
2,200	Palearctic	2,210	2,220	2,230	2,240	2,250	2,260
3,200	Neotropical-Antarctican	3,210	3,220	3,230	3,240	3,250	3,260
4,200	Indomalayan (Oriental)	4,210	4,220	4,230	4,240	4,250	4,260
5,200	African (Afrotropical)	5,210	5,220	5,230	5,240	5,250	5,260
6,200	Australian	6,210	6,220	6,230	6,240	6,250	6,260
7,200	Oceanic	7,210	7,220	7,230	7,240	7,250	7,260

*Swamp forests, bog forests, and riparian forests.

Upland (Terrestrial) Formations

Tundra—Arctic and alpine communities existing in an environment so cold that moisture is unavailable during most of the year, precluding the establishment of trees, and in which the maximum vegetative development is perennial herbaceous plants, shrubs, lichens, and mosses, with grasses poorly represented or at least not dominant. We nonetheless recognize that the holistic integrity of a "tundra" formation-type is open to serious question. Tundra may also be treated as composed of scrublands, grasslands, desertlands, and marshlands (wet-tundra) existing in an Arctic-Boreal climatic zone (Billings and Mooney 1968; Billings 1973). Alpine tundra communities in the Neotropics are known as Páramos.

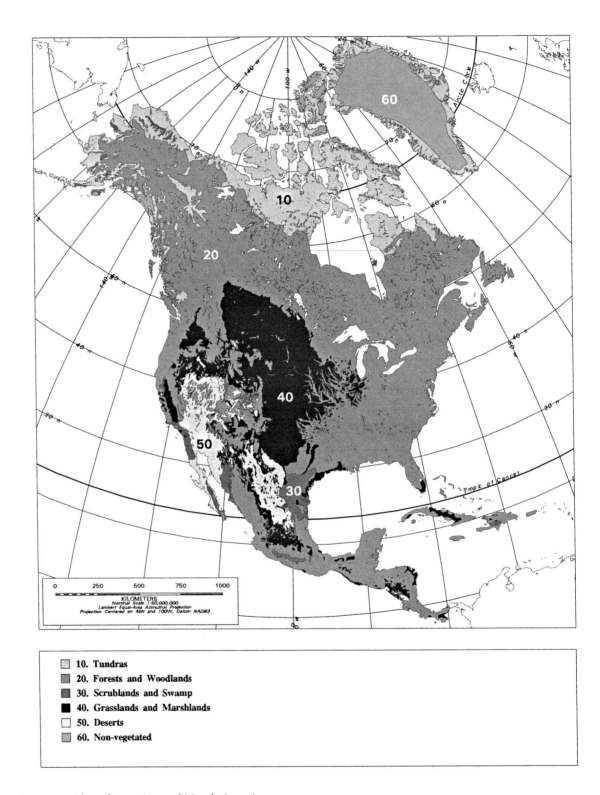

10. Tundras
20. Forests and Woodlands
30. Scrublands and Swamp
40. Grasslands and Marshlands
50. Deserts
60. Non-vegetated

Figure 3. Plant formations of North America.

Forest and Woodland—Communities dominated principally by trees actually or potentially more than ten meters in height, and characterized by closed and/or multi-layered canopies (forests); or, communities comprised principally of trees with a mean actual or potential height usually less than ten meters, the canopy of which is open, interrupted, and singularly layered (woodland). The "savanna" formation-type of some biogeographers (e.g., Beard 1953; Dyksterhuis 1957) is here recognized as a grassland. We follow the UNESCO classification system in which savannas are areas having an almost continual grass cover, and in which trees may form up to 30 percent of the plant cover (Mueller-Dombois and Ellenberg 1974). "Parklands," mosaics of grassland and smaller or larger stands of trees or shrubs, are considered as being represented by two or more distinct formation-types.

Scrubland—Communities dominated by shrubs and/or multistemmed trees generally not exceeding ten meters in height, often possessing microphyll or sclerophyll leaves, usually presenting a closed physiognomy, or, if open, interspaced with low-structured perennials.

Grassland—Communities dominated actually or potentially by grasses and/or other herbaceous plants.

Desertland—Communities in an arid environment (usually less than 300 millimeters precipitation per annum) in which more than 50 percent of the ground can be expected to lack vegetative cover.

Wetland Formations

Wet Tundra—Wetland communities existing in an environment so cold that plant moisture is unavailable during most of the year, precluding the establishment of trees and all but a low herbaceous plant structure in a hydric matrix. Wet tundra may also be treated as swampscrub, marshland, or strand communities within an Arctic-Boreal climatic zone.

Swamp and Riparian Forest—Wetland communities possessing an overstory of trees potentially more than ten meters in height and frequently characterized by closed and/or multi-layered canopies.

Swamp and Riparian Scrub—Wetland communities dominated by short trees and/or woody shrubs, generally under ten meters in height and usually presenting a closed physiognomy.

Marshland—Wetland communities in which the principal emergent plant cover consists of herbaceous emergents having their basal portions annually, periodically, or continually submerged.

Strand—Beach and river channel communities subject to regular to infrequent submersion, wind-driven waves, or spray. Plants are separated by significant areas devoid of perennial vegetation and the vegetative cover is usually less than 50 percent.

Some upland and wetland communities, e.g., dunes, lava flows, glaciers, salt lakes, etc., are essentially without vegetation. For purposes of classification, such areas can be considered as belonging to a nonvegetated or a "nonvascular plant formation" if a desertland or strand formation-type is considered inappropriate (table 2).

Third Level   The third digit beyond the comma (e.g., 1,11<u>1</u>) refers to one of the four world **climatic zones** (see, e.g., Walter 1973, Ray 1975, and Cox, Healey, and Moore 1976) in which minimum temperatures are recognized as a major evolutionary control of and within formation types (table 3, fig. 4).

Arctic-Boreal (Antarctic-Austral)—Lengthy periods of freezing temperatures with the coldest month isotherm -3°C. (Köppen 1931); growing season generally averaging less than 100 days, occasionally interrupted by nights of below-freezing temperatures.

Cold Temperate—Freezing temperatures usually of moderate duration, although of frequent occurrence during winter months. Potential growing season generally from 100 to 200 days and confined to late spring and summer when freezing temperatures are infrequent or absent.

Warm Temperate—Freezing temperatures of short duration but generally occurring every year during winter months. Potential growing season more than 200 days with less than an average of 150 days a year subject to temperatures below 0°C. or chilling fogs.

Tropical-Subtropical—Infrequent or no twenty-four-hour periods of freezing temperatures, cold fogs, or chilling winds.

Fourth Level   The fourth digit after the comma (e.g., 1,111.<u>1</u>) refers to a regional formation *within* a biotic province. Each of these **biotic communities** comes with a name that describes the formation's ecological center and/or one of its most distinguishing physiographic features, e.g., "Chihuahuan Desertscrub." These names in turn are derived from the biotic province in which the biotic community is found.

Also called biogeographic regions, biotic provinces are areas characterized by a particular precipitation pattern or other climatic regimen so that the plant and animal species found therein share a more or less similar environment (Vestal 1914; Ruthven 1920; Clements and Shelford 1939; Pitelka 1941; Dice 1943; Odum 1945; Goldman and Moore 1945; Blair 1950; Webb 1950; Miller 1951; Kendeigh 1952; Ryan 1963; Lowe 1964; Aldrich 1967; Franklin 1977; and, most recently, Udvardy 1975a, 1975b, 1984a, 1984b). As used here, biotic provinces are regional areas having a distinctive recent evolutionary history and hence a more or less characteristic biota at the species and subspecies levels. Similar regions classified solely on the basis of vegetation or fauna are called phytogeographic and faunistic provinces respectively (Lowe 1964). Composed of one or more formation-classes, biotic provinces can be subdivided into districts (Dice 1943; Blair 1950) as well as into biotic communities (Brown 1982). The "Ecoregion" and "Ecosystem" classifications recently proposed for the United States and Canada (see, e.g., Bailey and Cushwa 1981, Wiken, Rubec, and Ironside 1989, Demarchi 1993, and Ricketts et al. 1997), while based more on geographic criteria than on evolutionary considerations, are roughly analogous to biotic provinces. Their respective "province" and "ecoprovince" levels are more similar, however, to biotic districts than to biotic communities.

Table 3. Summary for the natural upland and wetland vegetation of Nearctic and Neotropical North America to the third level

Formation-type		Climatic (thermal) Zone			
		Arctic-Boreal Antarctic-Austral	Cold Temperate	Warm Temperate	Tropical-Subtropical
NEARCTIC					
Upland					
1,110	Tundra	1,111			
1,120	Forest and Woodland	1,121	1,122	1,123	1,124
1,130	Scrubland	1,131	1,132	1,133	1,134
1,140	Grassland	1,141	1,142	1,143	1,144
1,150	Desertland	1,151	1,152	1,153	1,154
1,160	Nonvegetated	1,161	1,162	1,163	1,164
Wetland					
1,210	Wet Tundra	1,211			
1,220	Swamp and Riparian Forests	1,221	1,222	1,223	1,224
1,230	Swamp and Riparian Scrublands	1,231	1,232	1,233	1,234
1,240	Marshland	1,241	1,242	1,243	1,244
1,250	Strand	1,251	1,252	1,253	1,254
1,260	Nonvegetated	1,261	1,262	1,263	1,264
NEOTROPICAL					
Upland					
3,110	Tundra and Páramo	3,111			
3,120	Forest and Woodland	3,121	3,122	3,123	3,124
3,130	Scrubland	3,131	3,132	3,133	3,134
3,140	Grassland	3,141	3,142	3,143	3,144
3,150	Desertland and Puna	3,151	3,152	3,153	3,154
3,160	Nonvegetated	3,161	3,162	3,163	3,164
Wetland					
3,210	Wet Tundra	3,211			
3,220	Swamp and Riparian Forests	3,221	3,222	3,223	3,224
3,230	Swamp and Riparian Scrublands	3,231	3,232	3,233	3,234
3,240	Marshland	3,241	3,242	3,243	3,244
3,250	Strand	3,251	3,252	3,253	3,254
3,260	Nonvegetated	3,261	3,262	3,263	3,264

Some biotic provinces and biotic communities have long been recognized by ecologists, and their designations, if not their boundaries, are widely accepted, for example, the Sonoran Desert (Shreve 1942, 1951; MacMahon 1988), Plains Grassland (Weaver and Clements 1938; Sims 1988), California Chaparral (Munz and Keck 1949, 1950), Arctic Tundra (Bliss 1988), and Northeastern Deciduous Forest (Braun 1950; Greller 1988). Others, for example, Alaskan Tundra (Shelford 1963; Ricketts et al. 1997), Madrean Evergreen Woodland (Lowe 1964; Brown 1982), and Sinaloan Deciduous Forest (Gentry 1982), are in the process of being adopted. Still other communities, including those in the Guatemalan, Veracruz, and Yucatán biotic provinces, have yet to be accepted or adequately tested.

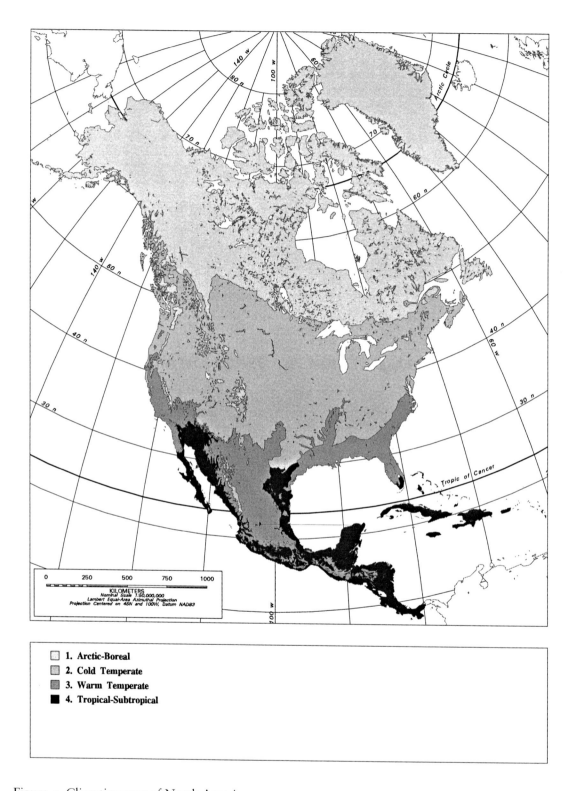

☐ 1. Arctic-Boreal
▨ 2. Cold Temperate
▩ 3. Warm Temperate
■ 4. Tropical-Subtropical

Figure 4. Climatic zones of North America.

The biotic provinces shown in figure 5 are modifications and refinements of those proposed by Goldman and Moore (1945), Ryan (1963), Udvardy (1975a, 1975b), and others, and neither their terminology nor their boundaries are intended to be final. The following descriptions for the provinces of the Nearctic Realm are therefore tentative, and intended solely to facilitate the completion of the classification system:

Polar (e.g., Polar Tundra, Polar Wetlands, etc.): This is essentially the high-arctic region of Bliss (1988) and other ecologists, and consists of those regions lying mostly above 72 degrees N latitude and characterized by an extremely harsh climate, low precipitation, and more or less continuous permafrost.

Alaskan-Yukon (e.g., Alaskan Tundra, Alaska-Yukon Subarctic Conifer Forest, Alaskan Swamp Scrub, Alaskan Wet Tundra, etc.): Northern and western coastal Alaska, interior Alaska, and most of Yukon Territory (the "Alaskan Tundra" and "Yukon Taiga" of Udvardy 1975a, 1975b).

Canadian (e.g., Canadian Tundra, Canadian Taiga, Canadian Marshland, etc.): Boreal Canada and the northeastern United States south of the High-Arctic and the Alaska-Yukon biotic provinces, including a number of offshore islands. The mean annual growing season is less than 100 days and most of the precipitation falls as snow. Udvardy's (1975a, 1975b) "Canadian Taiga" and "Canadian Tundra."

Arctic-Alpine (e.g., Arctic-Alpine Tundra): Mountainous areas above timberline that lie within and adjacent to the Alaskan-Yukon and Canadian biotic provinces.

Greenlandian (e.g., Greenlandian Coastal Tundra, Greenlandian Wet Tundra, etc.): Coastal Greenland and offshore islands not covered by ice and not subject to permafrost (see also Udvardy 1975a, 1975b).

Rocky Mountain (e.g., Rocky Mountain Alpine Tundra, Rocky Mountain Subalpine Conifer Forest, Rocky Mountain Montane Conifer Forest, Rocky Mountain Montane Meadow, Rocky Mountain Riparian Deciduous Forest, etc.): The Rocky Mountain cordillera from British Columbia southward to the higher elevations of the Chiricahua Mountains in Arizona. Also included here are the upper elevations of those mountains within the Great Basin biotic province (see also, e.g., Udvardy 1975a, 1975b, and Peet 1988).

Cascade-Sierran (e.g., Cascade-Sierran Alpine Tundra, Cascade-Sierran Subalpine Conifer Forest, Cascade-Sierran Montane Conifer Forest, Cascade-Sierran Montane Chaparral, etc.): Communities residing in the higher elevations of the Cascade and Sierra Nevada mountain cordillera from British Columbia southward through the Sierra Nevada and the Transverse and Peninsular ranges to the Sierra San Pedro de Martir in Baja California Norte (see also Udvardy 1975a, 1975b).

Adirondack-Appalachian (e.g., Adirondack-Appalachian Alpine Tundra, Adirondack-Appalachian Subalpine Conifer Forest, etc.): High-elevation communities in the Adirondack and Appalachian

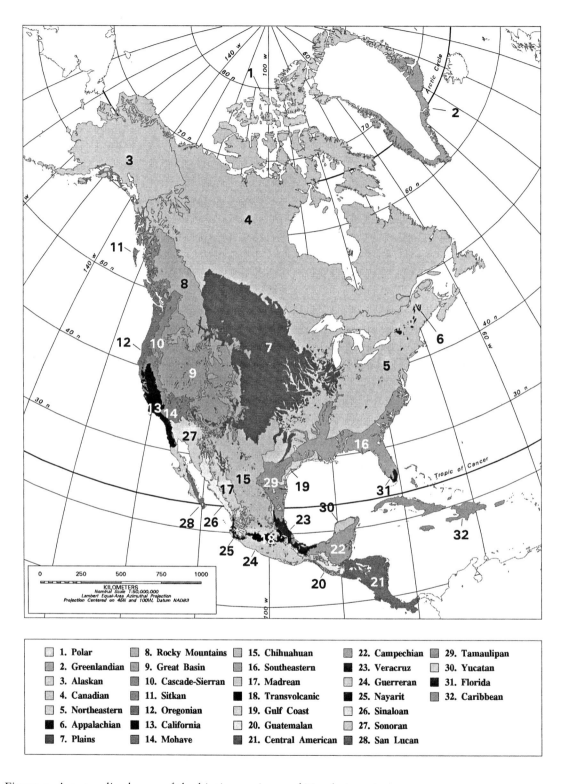

Figure 5. A generalized map of the biotic provinces of North America.

mountain cordillera from Maine and New Brunswick southward to the Great Smoky Mountains in Tennessee and North Carolina.

Transvolcanic (e.g., Transvolcanic Alpine Tundra, Transvolcanic Subalpine Conifer Scrubland, Transvolcanic Subalpine Grassland, etc): Those high-elevation communities along the Eje Volcano cordillera of Central Mexico—the "Transverse Volcanic" biotic province of Goldman and Moore (1945).

Northeastern (e.g., Northeastern Deciduous Forest, Northeastern Maritime Marshland, etc.): The cold temperate and summer wet "Eastern Deciduous Forest" of Braun (1950) and Greller (1988) minus the Mixed Deciduous and Evergreen Forest region in the warm-temperate southeastern United States. The "Eastern Forest" of Udvardy (1975a, 1975b).

Sitka Coastal (e.g., Sitkan Coastal Conifer Forest, Sitkan Coastal Strand, etc.): Those rain- and fog-drenched communities in the cismontane region of the Pacific coast from the vicinity of Vancouver Island northwestward to southern Alaska. The "Sitkan" biotic province of Dice (1943); the "Sitkan" biogeographical province of Udvardy (1975a, 1975b).

Oregonian (e.g., Oregonian Coastal Conifer Forest, Oregonian Deciduous and Evergreen Forest, Coastal Grassland, Oregonian Maritime Marshland, etc.): Cismontane communities occurring between the Pacific Coast and the Cascade and coast ranges from the vicinity of Vancouver Island southward to the San Francisco Bay region of central California, and locally, southward. The "Oregonian" biotic province of Dice (1943) and the "Oregonian" biogeographical province of Udvardy (1975a, 1975b).

Great Basin, or Intermountain (e.g., Great Basin Conifer Woodland, Great Basin Montane Scrub, Great Basin Shrub-Grassland, Great Basin Interior Marshland, etc.): Those relatively highelevation intermountain communities between the Rocky Mountain and Cascade-Sierran cordilleras. The "Artemisian," "Palusian," and "Navahonian" biotic communities of Dice (1943); Udvardy's (1975a, 1975b) "Great Basin" biogeographic province.

Plains (e.g., Plains Grassland, Plains Interior Marshland, etc.): Those cold-temperate communities lying west of the Northeastern Deciduous Forest, east of the Rocky Mountain cordillera, and south of the Canadian Taiga. The northern portions of Udvardy's (1975a, 1975b) "Grasslands" biogeographic province.

Southeastern (e.g., Southeastern Deciduous and Evergreen Forest, Southeastern Maritime Scrubland, Southeastern Riparian Forest, etc.): Those mostly forested warm-temperate communities south and southeast of the cold-temperate Northeastern Deciduous Forest exclusive of the Texas and western Louisiana Gulf Coast and those tropical communities peculiar to extreme southern Florida. Braun's (1950) "Southeastern Evergreen Forest" region, Dice's (1943) "Austroriparian" biotic province, Udvardy's (1975a, 1975b) "Austroriparian" biogeographic province, and Christensen's (1988) "Southeastern Coastal Plain."

Gulf Coastal (e.g., Gulf Coastal Grassland, Gulf Coastal Maritime Marshland): Those open, or formerly open, grassland and wetland communities found along the Texas and western Louisiana coasts. Tharp's (1939) "Coastal Prairie."

California (e.g., California Evergreen Forest and Woodland, California Chaparral, California Coastalscrub, California Valley Grassland, California Interior Marshland, etc.): Those warm-temperate, winter-rainfall communities west of the Sierra Nevada and Peninsula ranges, south and east of the Oregonian biotic province's coastal forests, and north of the Sonoran Desert in Baja California Norte. The "Californian" biotic province of Dice (1943), Udvardy (1975a, 1975b), and other authors.

Madrean (e.g., Madrean Montane Conifer Forest, Madrean Montane Meadow, Madrean Evergreen Woodland, etc.): Those moderate- to high-elevation communities found in the mountains and foothills of the Sierra Madre Oriental, the Sierra Madre Occidental, and their outliers (Brown 1982). The "Sierra Madre Occidental" and "Sierra Madre Oriental" biotic provinces of Goldman and Moore (1945) and the northern portions of Udvardy's (1975a, 1975b) "Madrean-Cordilleran" biogeographic province.

Guerreran (e.g., Guerreran Evergreen Forest and Woodland). Temperate communities at moderate to high elevations in the Sierra Madre del Sur and other mountain ranges south of the Rio Balsas and west of the Isthmus of Tehuantepec. The "Sierra Madre del Sur" biotic province of Goldman and Moore (1945); portions of Udvardy's (1975a, 1975b) "Madrean-Cordilleran" biogeographic province.

Guatemalan (e.g., Guatemalan Montane Conifer Forest, Guatemalan Evergreen Forest and Woodland): Those temperate and moderate- to high-elevation communities east of the Isthmus of Tehuantepec in Chiapas, Mexico; Guatemala; Honduras; and northern Nicaragua. Goldman and Moore's (1945) "Chiapas Highlands" and Ryan's (1963) "Chiapas-Guatemala Altos," "Lempira-Tegucigalpan," and "Nicaraguan Montane" biotic provinces. The southern portion of Udvardy's (1975a, 1975b) "Madrean-Cordilleran" biogeographic province.

Veracruz (e.g., Veracruz Cloud Forest): Wet, warm-temperate hardwood forest communities found at moderate to high elevations east of the crest of the Sierra Madre Oriental and north of the Transvolcanic mountain ranges (see, e.g., Martin 1958).

San Lucan (e.g., San Lucan Evergreen Forest and Woodland): Those temperate communities in the Sierra de la Laguna and adjacent mountain ranges in the Cape region of Baja California Sur (Arriaga and Ortega 1988). The higher elevations of Dice's (1943) "San Lucan" biotic province.

Chihuahuan, or Semidesert (e.g., Chihuahuan Desertscrub, Chihuahuan Interior Chaparral, Semidesert Grassland, Chihuahuan Interior Marshland, etc.): Those arid and semi-arid communities on the Mexican Plateau between the Sierra Madre Oriental and the Sierra Madre Occidental, and north of the Eje Volcanoes. The northern boundaries are less determinate but extend into west Texas, southern New Mexico, and southeastern Arizona (Shreve 1942; Udvardy 1975a, 1975b; Morafka 1977; Brown 1982). This biotic province contains most of the "Chihuahuan" and "Apachian" biotic provinces of Dice (1943).

Mohave (e.g., Mohave Desertscrub, Mohave Interior Strand, etc.): Those warm-temperate communities lying within the boundaries of the Mohave Desert (Shreve 1942; Turner 1982; Brown and Lowe 1980, 1994). Dice's (1943) "Mohavian" biotic province.

Southwestern Interior, or Arizona (e.g., Southwestern Interior Chaparral, Southwestern Riparian Deciduous Forest, etc.): Those warm-temperate and biseasonal-rainfall communities in sub-Mogollon Arizona and extreme western New Mexico north and east of the Sonoran Desert. Portions of Dice's (1943) "Navahonian," "Apachian," and "Sonora" biotic provinces. Further consideration may place these largely chaparral, grassland, and riparian communities within the Chihuahuan (Semidesert) biotic province (see, e.g., Brown 1982).

We have adopted the following biotic provinces in North America as occurring within the Neotropical Realm:

Central American (e.g., Central American Páramo, Central American Cloud Forest, Central American Evergreen Rain Forest, Central American Semi-evergreen Forest, Central American Dry (Monsoon) Forest, Central American Savanna Grassland, Central American Thornscrub, etc.): Panama, Costa Rica, El Salvador, and tropical Honduras and Nicaragua south of the Gulf of Honduras and below the Guatemalan highlands. Ryan's (1963) "Colón-Darien," "Guatuso-Talmanacan," "Chinandegan," "Mosquito," and "Escuinta-Usulután" biotic provinces. Udvardy's (1975a, 1975b) "Panamanian" and "Central American" biogeographic provinces.

Campechian (e.g., Campechian Semi-Evergreen Forest, Campechian Montane Evergreen Forest). The wet-tropic areas of southern Mexico, Guatemala, and Belize east of the Isthmus of Tehuantepec and below the Chiapas-Guatemalan highlands northward to the southern half of the Yucatán Peninsula. The southern portion of Goldman and Moore's (1945) and Ryan's (1963) "Yucatán Peninsula" biotic province; the southern half of Udvardy's (1975a, 1975b) "Campechian" biogeographic province.

Yucatán (e.g., Yucatán Semi-Deciduous Forest, Yucatán Dry Deciduous Forest, Yucatán Maritime Scrubland, etc.): The arid northern portions of the Yucatán Peninsula. The northern portion of the "Yucatán Peninsula" biotic province of Goldman and Moore (1945) and Udvardy's (1975a, 1975b) "Yucatecan" biogeographic province.

Guerreran, or Nayarit-Guerreran (e.g., Guerreran Dry Deciduous Forest, Guerreran Thornscrub, Nayarit-Guerreran Semi-Evergreen Forest, etc.): Those arid and semi-arid tropical valley and foothill communities occurring southward from Mexico's transverse volcanic ranges to the Isthmus of Tehuantepec and into the interior valleys of

Chiapas and Guatemala. This biotic province is essentially an expansion of the "Nayarit-Guerrero" biotic province of Goldman and Moore (1945) and is analogous to the "Guerreran" biogeographic province of Udvardy (1975a, 1975b).

Veracruz (e.g., Veracruz Evergreen Rain Forest, Veracruz Semi-Evergreen Forest, etc). Tropical and subtropical Mexico east of the Sierra Madre Oriental from the vicinity of Tampico south to the lowlands surrounding the northern portion of the Isthmus of Tehuantepec. The "Veracruz" biotic province of Goldman and Moore (1945).

Tamaulipan (e.g., Tamaulipan Semi-Deciduous Forest, Tamaulipan Thornscrub, Tamaulipan Coastal Strand, etc.): Those semi-arid subtropical and tropical communities found in southern Texas and northeastern Mexico southward to the vicinity of Tampico. The "Tamaulipan" biotic province of Dice (1943), Goldman and Moore (1945), Muller (1947), Martin (1958), and others.

Sinaloan (e.g, Sinaloan Dry Deciduous Forest, Sinaloan Thornscrub, Sinaloan Maritime Scrub, etc.): Those semi-arid subtropical and tropical communities west of the Sierra Madre Occidental and south and southeast of the Sonoran Desert from northeastern Sonora southward to the vicinity of Puerta Vallarta and the Transverse volcanic ranges. This province includes Shreve's (1951) "Foothills of Sonora" subdivision of the Sonoran Desert, Gentry's (1942, 1982) "Sinaloan Deciduous Forest," Goldman and Moore's (1945) "Sinaloa" biotic province, and the mainland portion of Udvardy's (1975a, 1975b) "Sinaloan" biogeographic province.

Sonoran (e.g., Sonoran Desertscrub, Sonoran Savanna Grassland, Sonoran Oasis Forests, etc.): Those communities contained within Shreve's (1942, 1951) boundaries of the Sonoran Desert in southeast California, Baja California, Arizona, and Sonora, save for his "Foothills of Sonora" subdivision. The "Sonora" biotic province of Goldman and Moore (1945) and the "Sonoran" biogeographic province of Udvardy (1975a, 1975b).

San Lucan (e.g., San Lucan Dry Deciduous Forest, San Lucan Thornscrub, etc.): The tropical and semi-arid portion of the Baja California Peninsula that is not Sonoran Desertscrub (see, e.g., Shreve 1951). The southern reaches of Dice's (1943) "San Lucan" biotic province and Goldman and Moore's (1945) "Southern Baja California" biotic province. The Baja Peninsular portion of Udvardy's (1975a, 1975b) "Sinaloan" biogeographic province.

Floridian (e.g., Floridian Evergreen [Hammock] Forest, Floridian Freshwater Marshland, Floridian Maritime Swamp Scrub, etc.): The southern extremity of the Florida Peninsula including the Florida Keys and adjacent waters. Portions of Udvardy's (1975a, 1975b) "Everglades" biogeographic province.

Caribbean (e.g., Caribbean Cloud and Montane Evergreen Forests, Caribbean Lowland Evergreen and Semi-evergreen Forest, Caribbean Dry Forest, Caribbean Thornscrub, Caribbean Savanna Grassland, Caribbean Coastal Strand, etc.): The West Indies including all of the islands of the Caribbean Sea north of Trinidad and Tobago. Further consideration may warrant the division of this biotic province into "Cuban," "Greater Antillean," and "Lesser Antillean" provinces as delineated by Udvardy (1975a, 1975b).

In the western United States, in Mexico, and in Central America, where the topographic relief is pronounced, climatic change and other ecologically isolating factors are more complex. Biotic communities in these areas therefore tend to diminish in size and increase in number. Their boundaries, following certain topographical features, may be sharply defined or highly complicated (Udvardy 1969). Even though the recognition of biotic communities will always be interpretive in part, their boundaries can be delineated by assigning communities of plant dominants and their associates (fifth level of the classification system) to the biotic province in which these species are characteristic taxa.

Biotic communities are characterized by distinctive plants and animals living within a formation-type (second level of the classification system) that are commonly called "indicator species" (Merriam and Stejneger 1890; Clements 1920; Shelford 1963). Because each biotic community is a complete ecosystem of plants, animals, and their habitats, this level is the natural unit for studying the interrelations of plant and animal species (Odum 1945; Shelford 1945; Kendeigh 1952). Although the original concept of "ecosystems" involved the exchange of chemical energy within a given community (Odum 1945), this term, as it is often presently used, is equivalent to a biotic community (see, e.g., MacKinnon et al. 1992). The reality of biotic communities as ecological units of regional isolation can be tested statistically through the analysis of climatic data and the presence (or absence) of endemics, as is presently being done for the San Lucan Dry Deciduous Forest by Breceda et al. (1994).

Each biotic community is analogous to a "small biome" in the biome hierarchy of Allen and Hoekstra (1992), in which vegetation can be seen as an exemplar of a community that contains both plants and animals. Viewed thus, plants and animals not only are members of a species, they are interacting members of a community. But, because they are composed of individual members, a biotic community is not in a progression toward stability in the Clementian sense, but is instead a complex that is subject to change with shifts in climate, the occurrence of "creative catastrophes" such as fire and hurricanes, and variations in animal numbers and pressures (Holling 1995). For these reasons, biotic communities may alter between cycles of forest and grassland, or shrubland and grassland, each species evolving both independently and dependently of the community as a whole. Moreover, some communities will grow in size, while others shrink in extent (Betancourt, Van Devender, and Martin 1990; McClaran and Van Devender 1995). The result is a change in not only the community's plants and animals, but in the biotic community itself, some biotic communities disappearing while newer ones evolve. Other biotic communities may retain their basic integrity even though a number of their principal constituents become extinct (see, e.g., Graham et al. 1996).

A complication frequently overlooked is that most biotic provinces contain more than one formation-type and hence more than one biotic community. For example, one can find grassland "savannas" within the Southeastern Deciduous and Evergreen Forest and "elfin" woodlands and "krumholtz" scrublands above tropical montane forests and subalpine forests. Although minor in extent, these often edaphic-controlled or otherwise limited communities have a distinctive evolutionary history and may justifiably be considered as biotic communities in their own right.

The fourth (biotic community) and fifth (series) levels have been most often used to map regions, states, and countries (e.g., Bruner 1931; Rasmussen 1941; Hayward 1948; Webb 1950; Allred, Beck, and Jorgensen 1963; Aldrich 1967; Küchler 1964, 1977; Franklin and Dyrness 1973; Brown 1973; Brown and Lowe 1980, 1994). Biotic provinces and biotic communities are also the bases for biosphere reserve programs in the United States and elsewhere (IUCN 1974, 1992; Franklin 1977; Udvardy 1984b).

Tables 4 and 5 list and illustrate those biotic communities shown on the 1:10,000,000 color map as well as a few others too minor in extent to depict. Present plans are to describe each of these biotic communities in a publication similar to one for the southwestern United States and northwestern Mexico (Brown 1982). Neither the classification nor the map is meant to be final. Additional biotic communities may be identified and some of those listed may be discarded upon further analysis and consideration.

Fifth Level   The fifth digit beyond the comma (e.g., 1,111.1$\underline{1}$) provides the principal plant-animal **series** within the biotic communities, each recognized by one or more indicator plants. These general series of actual or potential plant dominants, sometimes referred to as cover-types (Society of American Foresters 1954) or "alliances" (Nature Conservancy 1994a), are in turn composed of one or more plant associations (Oosting 1956; Lowe 1964; Braun 1950; Franklin and Dyrness 1973; Pfister et al. 1977). For example, a yellow-pine series would include all plant associations within a biotic community in which *Pinus ponderosa* is, or can be assumed to become, a dominant component (table 4). Because the number of series within any given biotic community may be large, and because some biotic communities are as yet little studied and imperfectly known, only illustrative examples of the fifth level are given for the biotic communities listed in tables 4 and 5. For these same reasons, the numerical prefix given for a particular series is also illustrative and may be modified at will.

It should be noted that tropical and subtropical series are inherently more diverse than those in arctic-boreal and temperate biotic communities. Series in tropical and subtropical biotic communities frequently contain dozens if not hundreds of competing species of plants and animals per unit area. Arctic-boreal series typically contain only one or two plant dominants.

Series in arctic-boreal and temperate environments also tend to be larger in extent and fewer in number than those in the tropics. For these reasons the identification and classification of fifth-level communities tend to be more specific in Canada and the United States than in Mexico or Central America (compare, for example, the vegetative classifications of Halliday 1937, Küchler 1964, Braun 1950, and Franklin and Dyrness 1973, with those of Tosi 1969 and Rzedowski 1978).

Some plant dominants are highly facultative (able to live under more than one set of conditions in various growth forms), and the same species may be dominant in more than one formation-type. As an extreme example, mesquite (*Prosopis juliflora*) may be the dominant life-form in forest and woodland, scrubland, desertland, and even disclimax grassland formations. The distributions of some plant dominants also span more than one climatic zone, for example, mesquite, creosote-bush (*Larrea tridentata*), and the introduced saltcedar (*Tamarix parviflora*). The plant and animal associates of these sometime-dominants usually differ, however, when passing from one formation-type or climatic zone to another. Some generic dominants may also occur in more than one biotic community (e.g., *Larrea, Populus, Salix, Quercus*, etc.). Nonetheless, further investigation should show a significant change in plant and animal associates when passing from one biotic community to another. Furthermore, when the same species is present in more than one biotic community, the different populations can be expected to exhibit genetic and other differences as was demonstrated by Yang (1970) for *Larrea tridentata* in the Chihuahuan, Sonoran, and Mohave deserts.

Sixth Level   The sixth digit after the comma (e.g., 1,111.11$\underline{1}$) refers to a distinctive **association**. An association has been defined by the International Botanical Congress in 1910 as a plant community having a particular floristic composition, uniform habitat conditions, and uniform physiognomy (see also, e.g., Braun-Blanquet 1932). Plant associations are therefore more or less local in distribution, and, as used here, generally equivalent to niches (Pitelka 1941) or habitat-types as outlined by Daubenmire and Daubenmire (1968), Layser (1974), and Pfister et al. (1977). Although we provide plant-association examples for two fifth-level series within one fourth-level biotic community (Douglas-fir and Yellow Pine series within Rocky Mountain Montane Conifer Forest), the enormous numbers of possible sets preclude presentation for the continental treatments in tables 4 and 5. The number of plant associations may therefore be expanded to accommodate regional studies.

This level of the classification system emphasizes existing vegetation. As a working system, it accommodates, but does not stress, both subclimax and disclimax plant associations as well as potential (prevailing) natural vegetation (see, e.g., Clements 1916, Weaver and Clements 1938, Clements and Shelford 1939, Oosting 1956, Küchler 1964, Shreve 1951, and Whittaker 1978). Those plant associations judged to be subclimax or seral in nature can be indicated by an "s" as a superscript above the numerical code, e.g. 111.111ˢ. Similarly, those series and associations considered to be in a disclimax or a more or less permanent man-altered condition can be indicated by a "D" at the series (fifth) level or a "d" at the plant association level.

Seventh Level   The seventh digit after the comma (e.g., 1,111.111<u>1</u>) accommodates detailed assessment of composition, structure, density, or other quantitative determinations for plant and animal species within a plant association. Implementation of this level in the system is intended for intensive studies of limited areas or "stands" (e.g., Dick-Peddie and Moir 1970). No examples are therefore provided in tables 4 and 5.

Table 4. Nomenclature of upland biotic communities for Nearctic and Neotropical North America

---

The biotic communities (fourth level) are presented on the 1:10,000,000 color map. Some series (fifth level) and association (sixth level) examples are provided here for demonstration purposes and indicated by an asterisk (*). A plus sign (⁺) indicates biotic communities for which our incomplete knowledge precludes presentation of representative series and association examples.

1,000. NEARCTIC REALM
  1,100. Natural Upland Vegetation
    1,110. Tundra Formation
      1,111. Arctic and Alpine Tundra
        1,111.1 Polar (High Arctic) Tundra (plate 1)
          1,111.11 Sedge-Moss Series*
          1,111.12 Cushion Plant-Lichen Series*
        1,111.2 Alaskan Tundra (plate 2)
        1,111.3 Canadian (Low Arctic) Tundra (plate 3)
        1,111.4 Greenlandian Coastal Tundra (plate 4)
        1,111.5 Arctic Alpine Tundra (plate 5)
        1,111.6 Rocky Mountain and Great Basin Alpine Tundra (plate 6)[a]
        1,111.7 Cascade-Sierran Alpine Tundra (plate 7)
        1,111.8 Adirondack-Appalachian Alpine Tundra (plate 8)
        1,111.9 Transvolcanic Alpine Tundra (plate 9)
        1,111.1a Madrean (*Cerro Potos'*) Alpine Tundra (plate 10)
    120. Forest and Woodland Formation[b]
      121. Boreal and Subalpine Forest and Woodland
        121.1 Alaska-Yukon Subarctic Conifer Forest (plate 11)
        121.2 Canadian Taiga (plate 12)
          121.21 White Spruce–Balsam Fir Series*
          121.22 Black Spruce Series*
        121.3 Rocky Mountain and Great Basin Subalpine Conifer Forest (plate 13)
          121.31 Engelmann Spruce-Alpine Fir Series*
          121.32 Bristlecone Pine-Limber Pine Series*
        121.4 Cascade-Sierran Subalpine Conifer Forest (plate 14)

---

[a] Further consideration may warrant separation of this biotic community into Rocky Mountain and Great Basin biotic communities.

[b] The first "1" (in front of the comma and representing the Nearctic realm) is understood and dropped from this point onward for tabular convenience only.

121.41 Limber Pine–Lodgepole Pine Series*

121.42 Whitebark Pine Series*

121.43 Mountain Hemlock Series*

121.5 Adirondack-Appalachian Subalpine Conifer Forest (plate 15)

121.51 Red Spruce–Balsam Fir Series*

121.6 Madrean Subalpine Conifer Forest

121.61 Hartweg Pine Series*

121.7 Transvolcanic Subalpine Conifer Forest (plate 16)

121.71 Hartweg Pine Series*

121.72 Religious Fir Series*

122. Cold Temperate Forest and Woodland

122.1 Northeastern Deciduous Forest (plate 17)

122.11 Oak-Hickory Series*

122.12 Oak-Chestnut Series*

122.13 Beech-Maple Series*

122.14 Oak-Pine Series*

122.15 Maple-Basswood Series*

122.16 Hemlock–White Pine–Mixed Hardwood Series*

122.2 Sitka Coastal Conifer Forest (plate 18)

122.21 Sitka Spruce–Douglas Fir Series*

122.3 Oregonian Coastal Conifer Forest (plate 19)

122.31 Coast Redwood Series*

122.32 Douglas Fir Series*

122.33 Western Hemlock Series*

122.4 Oregonian Deciduous and Evergreen Forest (plate 20)

122.41 Mixed Mesophytic Series*

122.42 Oregon White Oak Series*

122.43 Big-cone Spruce Series*

122.5 Cascade-Sierran Montane Conifer Forest (plate 21)

122.51 Mixed Conifer Series*

122.52 Red Fir Series*

122.53 Pacific Silver Fir Series*

122.54 White Fir Series*

122.55 Yellow Pine Series*

122.6 Rocky Mountain Montane Conifer Forest (plate 22)

122.61 Douglas Fir–White Fir (Mixed Conifer) Series*

122.611 *Pseudotsuga menziesii* Association*

122.612 *Pseudotsuga menziesii–Abies concolor* Association*

122.613 *Pseudotsuga menziesii*–mixed conifer Association*

122.614 *Populus tremuloides* subclimax Association*

122.62 Yellow Pine Series*

122.621 *Pinus ponderosa* Association*

122.622 *Pinus ponderosa*–mixed conifer Association*

122.623 *Pinus ponderosa–Quercus gambelii* Association*

122.624 *Pinus ponderosa–Quercus arizonica* Association*

122.625 *Pinus ponderosa–Juniperus deppeana* Association*

122.626 *Pinus ponderosa–Abies concolor* Association*

122.627 *Pinus ponderosa–Pinus flexilis* Association*

122.628 *Populus tremuloides* subclimax Association*

122.63 Gambel Oak Series*
   122.631 *Quercus gambelii* Association*
122.7 Great Basin Conifer Woodland (plate 23)
   122.71 Pinyon-Juniper Series*
122.8 Madrean Montane Conifer Forest (plate 24)
   122.81 Douglas Fir–Mixed Conifer Series*
   122.82 Yellow Pine Series*
122.9 Transvolcanic Montane Conifer Forest (plate 25)
   122.91 Douglas Fir Series*
   122.92 Yellow Pine Series*
122.1a Guatemalan Montane Conifer Forest (plate 26)
   122.1a1 White Pine Series*

123. Warm Temperate Forest and Woodland
  123.1 Southeastern Deciduous and Evergreen Forest (plate 27)
    123.11 Mixed Mesophytic Series*
    123.12 Pine Series*
  123.2 California Evergreen Forest and Woodland (plate 28)
    123.21 Encinal (Oak) Series*
    123.22 Oak-Pine Series*
    123.23 Walnut Series*
  123.3 Madrean Evergreen Forest and Woodland (plate 29)
    123.31 Encinal (Oak) Series*
    123.32 Oak-Pine Series*
  123.4 Relict Conifer Forest (plate 30)
    123.41 Closed-cone Pine Series*
    123.42 Cypress Series*
  123.5 Transvolcanic Evergreen Forest and Woodland (plate 31)
    123.51 Mixed Encinal Series*
  123.6 Guerreran Evergreen Forest and Woodland (plate 32)
    123.61 Encinal Series*
  123.7 Guatemalan Cloud Forest (plate 33)
    123.71 Encinal–Mixed Hardwood Series*
  123.8 Guatemalan Evergreen Forest and Woodland (plate 34)
    123.81 Pine-Oak Series*
  123.9 Veracruz Cloud Forest (plate 35)
    123.91 Oak–Mixed Hardwood Series*
  123.1a San Lucan Evergreen Forest and Woodland (plate 36)
    123.1a1 Encinal Series*

130. Scrubland Formation
 131. Arctic-Boreal Scrubland
  131.1 Alaskan Coastal Scrub (plate 37)
   131.11 Birch-Willow Series*
  131.2 Canadian Subpolar Scrub (plate 38)
   131.21 Birch-Willow Series*
  131.3 Alaskan Alpine and Subalpine Scrub (plate 39)
   131.31 Willow Series*
  131.4 Rocky Mountain Alpine and Subalpine Scrub (plate 40)
   131.41 Willow Series*
   131.42 Spruce Elfinwood Series*
   131.43 Bristlecone Pine Elfinwood Series*

131.5 Cascade–Sierran Alpine and Subalpine Scrub (plate 41)
   131.51 Limber Pine–Lodgepole Pine Elfinwood Series*
   131.52 Whitebark Pine Elfinwood Series*
131.6 Adirondack–Appalachian Alpine and Subalpine Scrub (plate 42)
   131.61 Hobblebush Series*
131.7 Madrean Alpine and Subalpine Scrub (plate 43)
   131.71 Prostrate Pinyon Scrub*

132. Cold Temperate Scrubland
  132.1 Great Basin Montane Scrub (plate 44)
    132.11 Oak-Scrub Series*
    132.12 Mountain-Mahogany Series*
    132.13 Maple-Scrub Series*
    132.14 Serviceberry Series*
    132.15 Bitterbrush Series*
    132.16 Mixed Deciduous Series*
  132.2 Cascade-Sierran Montane Scrub
    132.21 Manzanita Series*
  132.3 Madrean Montane Scrub (plate 45)
  132.4 Plains Deciduous Scrub (plate 46)
    132.31 Oak-Scrub Series*
    132.32 Sumac Series*

133. Warm Temperate Scrubland
  133.1 California Chaparral (plate 47)
    133.11 Chamise Series*
    133.12 Scrub Oak Series*
    133.13 Manzanita Series*
    133.14 Ceanothus Series*
  133.2 California Coastalscrub (plate 48)
    133.21 Mixed Sage Series*
    133.22 Buckwheat Series*
  133.3 Southwestern Interior (Arizona) Chaparral (plate 49)
    133.31 Scrub Oak Series*
    133.32 Manzanita Series*
    133.33 Ceanothus Series*
  133.4 Chihuahuan Interior (Coahuila) Chaparral (plate 50)
    133.41 Scrub Oak Series*
  133.5 Southeastern Maritime Scrub (plate 51)
    133.51 Scrub Oak Series*

134. Tropical-Subtropical Scrubland[c]

140. Grassland Formation
141. Arctic-Boreal Grassland
  141.1 Alaskan Grassland (plate 52)
    141.11 Cottongrass Series*
  141.2 Rocky Mountain Alpine and Subalpine Grassland (plate 53)
    141.21 Mixed Bunchgrass Series*
  141.3 Cascade-Sierran Alpine and Subalpine Grassland (plate 54)
    141.31 Mixed Bunchgrass Series*
  141.4 Adirondack-Appalachian Subalpine Grassland
    141.41 Oatgrass-Herb Series*

[c] Included in the Neotropical realm in this classification.

[d] Included and mapped as "Polar Tundra" in this classification.

153.11 Creosotebush-White Bursage Series*

153.12 Blackbrush Series*

153.13 Mesquite Series*

153.14 Bladdersage Series*

153.15 Joshuatree Series*

153.16 Saltbush Series*

153.2 Chihuahuan Desertscrub (plate 66)

153.21 Creosotebush-Tarbush Series*

153.22 Whitethorn Series*

153.23 Sandpaperbush Series*

153.24 Mesquite Series*

153.25 Mixed Scrub-Succulent Series*

153.26 Saltbush Series*

154. Tropical-Subtropical Desertland

3,000. NEOTROPICAL REALM

3,100. Natural Upland Vegetation

3,110. Tundra and Páramo Formation

3,111. Alpine Páramo

3,111.1 Central American Páramo[+] (plate 67)

120. Forest and Woodland Formation[e]

124. Tropical-Subtropical Forest and Woodland

124.1 Central American Cloud Forest[+] (plate 68)

124.2 Central American Evergreen Rain Forest[+] (plate 69)

124.3 Central American Semi-Evergreen Forest[+] (plate 70)

124.4 Central American Dry Forest[+] (plate 71)

124.5 Campechian Montane Evergreen Forest[+] (plate 72)

124.6 Campechian Semi-Evergreen Forest[+] (plate 73)

124.7 Yucatán Semi-Deciduous Forest[+] (plate 74)

124.8 Yucatán Dry Deciduous Forest[+] (plate 75)

124.9 Guerreran Dry Deciduous Forest[+] (plate 76)

124.1a Veracruz Evergreen Rain Forest[+] (plate 77)

124.1b Veracruz Semi-Evergreen Forest[+] (plate 78)

124.1c Nayarit-Guerreran Semi-Evergreen Forest[+] (plate 79)

124.1d Sinaloan Dry Deciduous (Monsoon) Forest[+] (plate 80)

124.1e Tamaulipan Semi-Deciduous Forest[+] (plate 81)

124.1f San Lucan Dry Deciduous Forest[+] (plate 82)

124.1g Caribbean Cloud and Montane Evergreen Forest (plate 83)

124.1g1 Ocotea–Roble de Sierra Series*

124.1h Caribbean Lowland Evergreen and Semi-Evergreen Forest (plate 84)

124.1h1 Pine Series*

124.1h2 Palm Series*

124.1i Caribbean Dry Forest (plate 85)

124.1i1 Mixed Short Tree Series*

124.1j Floridian Evergreen (Hammock) Forest (plate 86)

124.1j1 Mixed Hardwood Series*

130. Scrubland Formation

134. Tropical-Subtropical Scrubland

[e] The first "3" (in front of the comma and representing the Neotropical realm) is understood and dropped from this point onward for tabular convenience.

134.1 Guerreran Thornscrub[+] (plate 87)

134.2 Sinaloan Thornscrub (plate 88)

   134.21 Mixed Deciduous Series*

134.3 Tamaulipan Thornscrub (plate 89)

   134.31 Mixed Deciduous Series*

   134.32 Mesquite Disclimax Series*

134.4 San Lucan Thornscrub[+] (plate 90)

134.5 Caribbean Thornscrub[+] (plate 91)

134.6 Central American Thornscrub[+] (plate 92)

140. Grassland Formation

  144. Tropical-Subtropical Grassland

    144.1 Central American Savanna Grassland[+] (plate 93)

    144.2 Guerreran Savanna Grassland[+] (plate 94)

    144.3 Campechian and Veracruz Savanna Grassland[+] (plate 95)

    144.4 Caribbean Savanna Grassland[+] (plate 96)

    144.5 Sonoran Savanna Grassland[+] (plate 97)

    144.6 Tamaulipan Savanna Grassland[+] (plate 98)

150. Desertland Formation

  154. Tropical-Subtropical Desertland

    154.1 Sonoran Desertscrub (plates 99 and 100)

      154.11 Creosotebush-White Bursage (Lower Colorado Valley) Series*

      154.12 Paloverde-Mixed Cacti (Arizona Upland) Series*

      154.13 Brittlebush-Ironwood (Plains of Sonora) Series*

      154.14 Copal-Torote (Central Gulf Coast) Series*

      154.15 Agave-Bursage (Vizcaíno) Series*

      154.16 Paloblanco-Agria (Magdalena Plain) Series*

      154.17 Saltbush Series*

Table 5. Nomenclature of wetland biotic communities for Nearctic and Neotropical North America

Some series (fifth level) examples are provided here for demonstration purposes and indicated by an asterisk (*). A plus sign (+) indicates biotic communities for which our incomplete knowledge precludes presentation of representative series and association examples.

1,000. NEARCTIC REALM
  1,200. Natural Wetland Vegetation
    1,210. Wet Tundra Formation
      1,211. Arctic Wet Tundra (plate 101)
        1,211.1 Polar (High Arctic) Wet Tundra
          1,211.11 Sedge-Moss Series*
          1,211.12 Rush Series*
        1,211.2 Greenlandian Wet Tundra
          1,211.21 Sedge-Moss Series*
        1,211.3 Alaskan (Coastal) Wet Tundra
          1,211.31 Sedge-Moss Series*
        1,211.4 Canadian (Low Arctic) Wet Tundra
          1,211.41 Sedge-Grass-Moss Series*
          1,211.42 Rush Series*
    220. Forest Formation[a]
      221. Boreal Swamp and Riparian Forest (plate 102)
        221.1 Canadian Swamp Forest
          221.11 Black Spruce–Tamarack Series*
          221.12 Willow-Alder Series*
      222. Cold Temperate Swamp and Riparian Forest (plate 103)
        222.1 Northeastern Bog, Swamp, and Riparian Forests
          222.11 White Cedar Series*
          222.12 Cottonwood-Willow Series*
          222.13 Ash-Maple Series*
        222.2 Plains and Great Basin Riparian Deciduous Forest
          222.21 Cottonwood-Willow Series*
        222.3 Oregonian (Pacific Coastal) Riparian Deciduous Forest
          222.31 Cottonwood-Willow Series*
        222.4 Cascade-Sierran Riparian Deciduous Forest
          222.41 Cottonwood-Willow Series*
          222.42 Mixed Broadleaf Series*
        222.5 Rocky Mountain Riparian Deciduous Forest
          222.51 Cottonwood-Willow Series*
          222.52 Mixed Broadleaf Series*
      223. Warm Temperate Swamp and Riparian Forests (plate 104)
        223.1 Southeastern Swamp and Riparian Forest
          223.11 Tupelo-Cypress Series*
          223.12 Southern White Cedar Series*
          223.13 Mixed Hardwood Series*
          223.14 Cottonwood-Willow Series*
        223.2 Southwestern Riparian Deciduous Forest and Woodland
          223.21 Cottonwood-Willow Series*
          223.22 Mixed Broadleaf Series*
        223.3 California Riparian Deciduous Forest and Woodland
          223.31 Cottonwood-Willow Series*
          223.32 Mixed Broadleaf Series*

---

[a] The first "1" in front of the comma and representing the Nearctic realm is understood and dropped from this point onward for tabular convenience only.

[b]   See Neotropical realm.

241.21 Sedge Series*
241.22 Rush Series*
241.3 Alaskan Interior Marshland
241.31 Sedge Series*
241.4 Alaskan Maritime (Coastal) Marshland
241.41 Sedge Series*
241.5 Canadian Interior Marshland
241.51 Sedge Series*
241.6 Canadian Maritime Marshland
241.61 Sedge Series*
241.7 Adirondack-Appalachian Alpine and Subalpine Marshland
241.71 Sedge Series*
241.8 Cascade-Sierran Alpine and Subalpine Marshland
241.81 Sedge Series*
241.9 Rocky Mountain Alpine and Subalpine Marshland
241.91 Sedge Series*
241.92 Rush Series*
241.93 Manna Grass Series*
242. Cold Temperate Marshland (plate 109)
242.1 Northeastern Interior Marshland
242.11 Sedge Series*
242.12 Rush Series*
242.13 Bur-Reed Series*
242.14 Cattail Series*
242.15 Bulrush Series*
242.16 Arrow-Arum Series*
242.17 Reed Canarygrass Series*
242.18 Waterlily Series*
242.2 Northeastern Maritime Marshland
242.21 Saltgrass Series*
242.3 Plains Interior Marshland
242.31 Sedge Series*
242.32 Rush Series*
242.4 Great Basin Interior Marshland
242.41 Sedge Series*
242.5 Oregonian Interior Marshland
242.51 Sedge Series*
242.6 Oregonian (Pacific Coastal) Maritime Marshland
242.61 Saltgrass Series*
242.62 Glasswort Series*
242.7 Cascade-Sierran Montane Marshland
242.71 Sedge Series*
242.8 Rocky Mountain Montane Marshland
242.81 Sedge Series*
242.82 Rush Series*
243. Warm Temperate Marshland (plate 110)
243.1 Southeastern Interior Marshland
243.11 Cattail Series*
243.2 Southeastern Maritime Marshland
243.21 Saltmarshgrass Series*
243.3 Gulf Coastal Maritime Marshland
243.31 Saltgrass Series*
243.4 Southwestern Interior Marshland
243.41 Sedge Series*
243.5 Mohave Interior Marshland

3,000. NEOTROPICAL REALM
  3,200. Neotropical Natural Wetland Vegetation[c]
    3,220. Forest Formation
      3,224. Tropical-Subtropical Swamp, Riparian, and Oasis Forest and Woodland (plates 114 and 115)
        224.1 Floridian Interior Swamp and Riparian Forest[d]
          224.11 Mixed Evergreen Series*
          224.12 Palm Communities*
        224.2 Floridian Maritime Swamp Forest
          224.21 Mangrove Series*
        224.3 Tamaulipan Interior Swamp and Riparian Forest
          224.31 Mixed Evergreen Series*
          224.32 Palm Series*
        224.4 Sonoran Riparian and Oasis Forest
          224.41 Palm Series*
          224.42 Mesquite Bosque Series*
          224.43 Cottonwood-Willow Series*
      234. Tropical-Subtropical Swamp and Riparian Scrub (plate 116)
        234.1 Floridian Interior Swamp Scrub
          234.11 Mixed Evergreen Series*
        234.2 Floridian Maritime Swamp Scrub
          234.21 Mangrove Series*
        234.3 Gulf Coastal Interior Swamp and Riparian Scrub
          234.31 Mixed Evergreen Series*
        234.4 Gulf Coastal Maritime Swampscrub
          234.41 Mangrove Series*
        234.5 Sonoran Riparian Scrub
          234.51 Mixed Scrub Series*
          234.52 Seepwillow Series
          234.53 Saltcedar Disclimax Series*
      244. Tropical-Subtropical Marshland (plate 117)
        244.1 Floridian Interior Marshland
          244.11 Cattail Series*
          244.12 Bulrush Series*
          244.13 Giant Reed Series*
          244.14 Sawgrass Series*
        244.2 Floridian Maritime Marshland
          244.21 Saltgrass Series*
        244.3 Gulf Coastal Interior Marshland
          244.31 Cattail Series*
          244.32 Bulrush Series*
          244.33 Giant Reed Series*
        244.4 Gulf Coastal Maritime Marshland
          244.41 Saltgrass Series*
        244.5 Sonoran Interior Marshland
          244.51 Cattail Series*
          244.52 Bulrush Series*
          244.53 Giant Reed Series*
          244.54 Threesquare Series*
      254. Tropical-Subtropical Strand (plate 118)
        254.1 Floridian Interior Strand+
        254.2 Floridian Maritime Strand+

[c] Neotropical examples are given only for those biotic communities occurring in the United States.
[d] The first "3" in front of the comma and representing the Neotropical realm is understood and dropped from this point onward for tabular convenience only.

254.3 Gulf Coastal Interior Strand[+]
254.4 Gulf Coastal Maritime Strand[+]
254.5 Sonoran Interior Strand
  254.51 Mixed Shrub Series*

3

The Biotic Communities of North America Map

The accompanying 1:10,000,000 color map (Reichenbacher, Franson, and Brown 1998) depicts the continent's major biotic communities (fourth level of the classification system) using Gaussen's (1953) ecological color-scheme that illustrates gradients in available plant moisture, heat, and cold. The base map was reproduced from an acetate overlay of a 1:8,000,000 Kümmerly and Frey stereographic chart, and the biotic communities delineated in eighty-three vinyl colors using as source data the maps, terminology, and descriptions found in the Literature Cited and Literature Consulted as well as our own field work.

The biotic communities shown depict regional formations within recognized biotic and floristic provinces as modified from Dice (1943), Goldman and Moore (1945), Shreve (1951), Rzedowski (1978), Barbour and Billings (1988), and other biogeographers. The boundaries and terminology of the various biotic communities, while derived from numerous works, are modeled after papers developed by the IUCN and UNESCO and proposed for use in the International Biosphere Reserve program (Udvardy 1984a, 1984b). Neither the biotic community designations nor their delineations are final. Eventually, it is hoped that the use of high-altitude imagery and other recently developed techniques (see, e.g., Loveland et al. 1991) will result in an improved depiction of the boundaries of these biotic resources.

Because of the limitations of scale, upland biotic communities such as Relict Conifer Forests and Central American Thornscrub, occupying individual areas less than ca. 100 square kilometers in size, are omitted from the map. Their enormous diversity, dynamic nature, and generally limited area also precluded illustration of all but the largest wetlands. The biogeographic affiliation of these or any other wetlands can be readily determined by referring to the upland biotic community within which they occur. It is expected that further research and peer review will result in improvements in the nomenclature and delineation of the biotic communities depicted, particularly those in Latin America.

Some potential users and reviewers have objected to the large uniform areas of Northeastern Deciduous Forest, Canadian Taiga, and Plains Grassland when compared to the smaller, more numerous biotic communities in Mexico and the American Southwest. This apparent discrepancy is real, however, at the biotic community level. For the reasons already stated, biotic diversity increases as one

travels westward and southward across the North American continent—a phenomenon long recognized by biologists (e.g., Simpson
1964, Kiester 1971, and Wilson 1974). Mexico, despite having only
11 percent of the land area of Canada and the United States, has
more species of mammals, birds, and reptiles and amphibians than
the two northern countries combined. One Mexican state, Chiapas,
has 8,250 known species of plants as compared to the much larger
(115,719 versus 74,000 square kilometers) and botanically rich
American state of Ohio, which has 2,700 species (Ramamoorthy et
al. 1993). It is only reasonable then to show the southern parts of
North America as possessing greater variation at the biotic community level than the northern and eastern portions of the continent
(Klopfer and MacArthur 1960; Fleming 1973; Wilson 1974).

Nonetheless, further research may show that one or more of the
biotic communities depicted are not sufficiently distinct to warrant
fourth-level separation. Future investigators, for example, may con-
clude that the Neotropical Realm's Guerreran Deciduous Forest is
not sufficiently different from Sinaloan Deciduous Forest to justify
separate biotic community status. Conversely, additional study may
support the division of the Caribbean Biotic Province into Greater
Antillean and Lesser Antillean provinces as proposed by Udvardy
(1975b). Also, should additional biotic detail be desired within a
major biotic community, future editions of the map can provide series or fifth-level community designations as was done for the Northeastern Deciduous Forest by Braun (1950) and for Sonoran
Desertscrub by Shreve (1951) and Brown and Lowe (1980, 1994).

The map has been digitized by the Environmental Protection
Agency's National Exposure Research Laboratory, Characterization
Research Division, Las Vegas, Nevada. Digitization will facilitate
modifying the map's biotic communities based on peer review and
allow for the possible overlay of land-use data. Digitization will also
facilitate the division of larger biotic communities such as the Northeastern Deciduous Forest and Plains Grassland into large general series, should such further subdivision be desired.

One immediate use of the map is for estimating the areas of
North America's biotic communities (table 6). Such information will
enable biologists to stratify their samples in a more meaningful way,
thereby improving the precision and efficiency of wildlife surveys. A
continental sample frame is especially useful for conducting breeding
dove and other migratory bird surveys similar to those presently
being coordinated by the U.S. Fish and Wildlife Service. Even more
important, knowing the areal extent of biotic communities permits a
better assessment and appreciation of those areas still remaining in a
natural state.

In summation, the purpose of the map is to illustrate the applicability of the classification system for inventorying the continent's biotic resources and to provide a sample frame for those interested in
stratifying natural history surveys. With the recent availability of
highly detailed aerial imagery, one could feasibly now also overlay
land-use, thus measuring the extent of those biotic communities re-

maining in a natural state. National park boundaries and other en-
hancements would also enable resource managers to identify those
biotic communities having protected status and determine which are
in need of additional protection. A biotic communities map also facilitates the evaluation of candidate areas for biosphere reserve and
wilderness status. Enhanced with land use information, such a map
can also assist in the interpretation of environmental change.

Table 6. Areas of North American biotic communities

Areas (in 1,000 square kilometers) were derived from the digital data of the Map of the Biotic Communities
of North America.

1,000. NEARCTIC REALM	21,720
1,100. Natural Upland Vegetation	21,416
1,110. Tundra Formation	
111. Arctic and Alpine Tundra	
111.1 Polar (High Arctic) Tundra	610
111.2 Alaskan Tundra	168
111.3 Canadian (Low Arctic) Tundra	2,262
111.4 Greenlandian Coastal Tundra	364
111.5 Arctic Alpine Tundra	486
111.6 Rocky Mountain–Great Basin Alpine Tundra	51
111.7 Cascade-Sierran Alpine Tundra	4
111.8 Adirondack-Appalachian Alpine Tundra	<1
111.9 Transvolcanic Alpine Tundra	<1
120. Forest and Woodland Formation	
121. Boreal and Subalpine Forest and Woodland	
121.1 Alaska-Yukon Subarctic Conifer Forest	919
121.2 Canadian Taiga	4,631
121.3 Rocky Mountain and Great Basin Subalpine Conifer Forest	396
121.4 Cascade-Sierran Subalpine Conifer Forest	55
121.5 Adirondack-Appalachian Subalpine Conifer Forest	17
122. Cold Temperate Forest and Woodland	
122.1 Northeastern Deciduous Forest	2,712
122.2 Sitka Coastal Conifer Forest	209
122.3 Oregonian Coastal Conifer Forest	124
122.4 Oregonian Deciduous and Evergreen Forest	36
122.5 Cascade-Sierran Montane Conifer Forest	149
122.6 Rocky Mountain Montane Conifer Forest	554
122.7 Great Basin Conifer Woodland	299
122.8 Madrean Montane Conifer Forest	37
122.9 Transvolcanic Montane Conifer Forest	6
122.1a Guatemalan Montane Conifer Forest	5

123. Warm Temperate Forest and Woodland

   123.1 Southeastern Deciduous and Evergreen Forest   630

   123.2 California Evergreen Forest and Woodland   62

   123.3 Madrean Evergreen Forest and Woodland   218

   123.5 Transvolcanic Evergreen Forest and Woodland   57

   123.6 Guerreran Evergreen Forest and Woodland   42

   123.7 Guatemalan Cloud Forest   15

   123.8 Guatemalan Evergreen Forest and Woodland   67

   123.9 Veracruz Cloud Forest   6

   123.1a San Lucan Evergreen Forest and Woodland   >1

130. Scrubland Formation

 132. Cold Temperate Scrubland

   132.1   Great Basin Montane Scrub   29

 133. Warm Temperate Scrubland

   133.1   California Chaparral   34

   133.2   California Coastalscrub   27

   133.3   Southwestern Interior Chaparral   11

   133.4   Chihuahuan Interior Chaparral   30

140. Grassland Formation

 142. Cold Temperate Grassland

   142.1   Plains Grassland   2,341

   142.2   Great Basin Shrub-Grassland   524

 143. Warm Temperate Grassland

   143.1   Chihuahuan (Semidesert) Grassland   508

   143.2   California Valley Grassland   71

   143.3   Gulf Coastal Grassland   52

150. Desertland Formation   836

 152. Cold Temperate Desertland

   152.1   Great Basin Desertscrub   332

 153. Warm Temperate Desertland

   153.1   Mohave Desertscrub   124

   153.2   Chihuahuan Desertscrub   380

 161. Permanent Ice and Snow   1,760

200. Nearctic Natural Wetland Vegetation   304

3,000. Neotropical Realm   1,847

 3,100. Natural Upland Vegetation   1,784

  3,110. Tundra and Páramo Formation

  111. Alpine Páramo

   111.1   Central American Páramo   <1

  120. Forest and Woodland Formation

   124. Tropical-Subtropical Forest and Woodland

    124.1   Central American Cloud Forest   15

    124.2   Central American Evergreen Rain Forest   161

Plate 1. Polar (High Arctic) Tundra (111.1) on Ellesmere Island, Northwest Territories, Canada. Note the low stature of the "heath" and the large areas of barren, stony ground. Photo courtesy of R. E. Hamburg, Travel Arctic, Government of the Northwest Territories.

Plate 2. Alaskan Tundra (111.2) of low-growing grasses and sedges on Denali (Mount McKinley) National Park and Preserve. The caribou are the Alaskan subspecies, *Rangifer tarandus granti*. National Park Service photo.

Plate 3. Canadian (Low Arctic) Tundra (111.3) west of Hudson Bay, just south of the town of Churchill in Manitoba, Canada. It is November and the only plants protruding through the snow cover are a few shrubby willows (*Salix* sp.) and a very open stand of stunted black spruce (*Picea mariana*). Immediately to the south lies the boreal forest or Canadian Taiga. Photo by D. E. Brown.

Plate 4. Greenlandian Coastal Tundra (111.4) and musk-oxen (*Ovibos moschatus*) near Sondre Strønfjord in southwest Greenland. Note the stature of the heath vegetation in comparison to plate 1. Photo taken in July 1995 by Melvin Marcus.

Plate 5. Arctic Alpine Tundra (111.5) and Dall sheep (*Ovis dalli*) in the Cathedral Mountains, Denali National Park and Preserve, Alaska. Note the large areas of bare ground in this open "Dryas-Lichen community" at ca. 1350 m (4430 ft) altitude. Photo by D. E. Brown.

Plate 6. Rocky Mountain Alpine Tundra (111.6) in the Rio Grande National Forest, Colorado, ca. 3,900 m (12,800 ft) altitude. It is midsummer and many of the alpine plants, which include *Kobresia myosuroides, Polygonum bistortoides, Trifolium nanum,* and *Geum rossi,* are in bloom. U. S. Forest Service photo taken by H. E. Schwan on August 8, 1945.

Plate 7. Cascade-Sierran Alpine Tundra (111.7) at ca. 2900 m (9500 ft) altitude in the Sierra Nevada, Washoe County, Nevada. Steep terrain and a windswept ridge inimical to tree growth allow this rocky-fell field of bare rock and prostrate shrubs to extend below the usual occurrence of alpine tundra in the Sierra Nevada. Photo taken by Richard E. Brown in September 1995.

Plate 8. Adirondack-Appalachian Alpine Tundra (111.8). A view of the summit area of Mount Washington in New Hampshire's White Mountains, ca. 1830 m (6000 ft) altitude. Several species of lichens and mosses are present in addition to a single species of sedge (*Carex bigelowii*) in this "rock-fell" habitat. Photo by D. E. Brown.

Plate 9. Transvolcanic Alpine Tundra (111.9). A view of the still active Volcán de Fumeral from the uppermost slopes of the Sierra de Colima in Jalisco, Mexico. The altitude is ca. 4250 m (13900 ft). In this open and depauperate alpine community at latitude 19 degrees North, the number of plant species present can literally be counted on one's fingers. Photo by D. E. Brown.

Plate 10. Madrean Alpine Tundra (111.1a) atop Cerro Potosí, Nuevo Leon, Mexico, at ca. 3700 m (12140 ft) populated by short-statured forbs such as *Potentilla leonina*, *Arenaria* sp., *Bidens muelleri*, *Lupinus cacuminis*, *Senecio scalaris*, and *Castilleia bella* (Beaman and Andresen 1966). The almost total lack of grasses in this "alpine meadow" may be at least partially due to grazing pressures (note dairy cattle in background). Photo by D. E. Brown.

Plate 11. Alaska-Yukon Subarctic Conifer Forest (121.1) consisting mostly of white spruce (*Picea glauca*) in Denali National Park and Preserve, Alaska. Photo by D. E. Brown.

Plate 12. Canadian Taiga (121.2). Boreal communities such as this virgin stand of black spruce (*Picea mariana*) in Minnesota's Big Falls Experimental Forest extend southward into the northern tier of U.S. states on poorly drained acidic soils. The understory is commonly a feathermoss, in this case probably *Pleurozium schreberi*. U. S. Forest Service photo by L. P. Neff.

Plate 13. Rocky Mountain Subalpine Conifer Forest (121.3) of Engelmann spruce *(Picea engelmanni)* and alpine fir (*Abies lasiocarpa*) at an altitude of ca. 2600 m (8500 ft) in the Arapaho National Forest in Colorado. U. S. Forest Service photo taken by E. S. Shipp in 1927.

Plate 14. Cascade-Sierran Subalpine Conifer Forest (121.4) in Olympic National Park, Washington. The trees at this altitude, which is ca. 1500 m (5000 ft), are mostly mountain hemlock (*Tsuga mertensiana*) and Pacific silver fir (*Abies amabilis*). National Park Service photo taken in 1934.

Plate 15. Adirondack-Appalachian Subalpine Conifer Forest (121.5). This virgin red spruce (*Picea rubens*) forest on Barton's Knob in the southern Appalachian Mountains near Durbin, West Virginia, is one of the southernmost fasciations of this biotic community. U. S. Forest Service photo taken in August 1939 by Leon S. Minckler.

Plate 16. Transvolcanic Subalpine Conifer Forest (121.7) of Hartweg pines (*Pinus hartwegii*), Montezuma pines (*Pinus montezumae*), and alder (*Alnus firmifolia)* extending from ca. 3050 m (10000 ft) altitude to timberline in the Sierra Nevada de Colima, Jalisco, Mexico. Photo by D. E. Brown.

Plate 17. Northeastern Deciduous Forest (122.1). This Beech (*Fagus grandifolia*)–Maple (*Acer saccharum*) series on the Bartlett Experimental Forest in New Hampshire is representative of but one of several major fasciations of this important and extensive biotic community. U. S. Forest Service photo taken in August 1938 by Victor S. Jensen.

Plate 18. Sitka Coastal Conifer Forest (122.2) dominated by Sitka spruce (*Picea sitchensis*) and western hemlock (*Tsuga heterophylla*) in the Tongass National Forest, Alaska. U. S. Forest Service photo taken by H. L. Shantz in June 1938.

Plate 19. Oregonian Coastal Conifer Forest (122.3) comprised of an old-growth stand of coast redwoods (*Sequoia sempervirens*) in Del Norte County, California. The man standing in the lower left of the photo indicates the size of these redwoods. Photo by Douglass P. Roy.

Plate 20. Oregonian Deciduous and Evergreen Forest (122.4) at Falling Springs in the San Gabriel Mountains—a southern fasciation of a mixed mesophytic series that extends from Oregon to southern California. Important trees at this 1220 m (4000 ft) altitude location in the Los Angeles National Forest are big-cone Douglas fir *(Pseudotsuga macrocapa)*, incense cedar (*Libocedrus decurrens*), and both evergreen oaks (e.g., *Quercus chrysolepis*) and a deciduous oak (*Quercus kelloggi*). Photo by D. E. Brown.

Plate 21. Cascade-Sierran Montane Conifer Forest (122.5) represented here by a virgin stand of red fir (*Abies magnifica*) in the Tahoe National Forest in California's Sierra Nevada. U.S. Forest Service photo taken by W. I. Hutchinson in 1935.

Plate 22. Rocky Mountain Montane Conifer Forest (122.6) consisting of an almost pure stand of old-growth ponderosa pines *(Pinus ponderosa)* with a bunch-grass understory in the White Mountains of Arizona. The altitude is ca. 2500 m (8200 ft). U.S. Forest Service photo taken in August 1957 by Daniel O. Todd.

Plate 23. Great Basin Conifer Woodland (122.7) of mostly Rocky Mountain juniper *(Juniperus scopulorum)* and Rocky Mountain pinyon *(Pinus edulis)* at an altitude of ca. 1800 m (5900 ft) southwest of Flagstaff, Arizona. U. S. Forest Service photo taken in 1920.

Plate 24. Madrean Montane Conifer Forest (122.8) at an altitude of ca. 2100 m (6900 ft) along the Sonora-Chihuahua border. The trees are almost entirely ponderosa pine *(Pinus ponderosa* var. *arizonica).* Photo taken by Dirk V. Lanning about 1979 while he was studying thick-billed parrots (*Rhynchopsitta pachyrhyncha*) in northern Mexico.

Plate 25. Transvolcanic Montane Conifer Forest (122.9) of Douglas fir *(Pseudotsuga menziesi)* at an altitude of ca. 2600 m (8530 ft) in the Sierra Angangueo, Michoacán, Mexico. This forest is the winter home of countless migrating monarch butterflies (*Danaus plexippus*), whose caterpillars feed on the milkweed (*Asclepias* sp.) understory. Photo by D. E. Brown.

Plate 26. Guatemalan Montane Conifer Forest (122.1a) at ca. 2600 m (8500 ft) altitude on the north slopes of Cerro Tecpán off the Pan American Highway northwest of Guatemala City. The trees are almost entirely Holarctic genera and include *Pinus ayacahuite, P. pseudostrobus, P. montezumae, Abies guatemalensis*, a cypress (*Cupressus* sp.), and an alder (*Alnus* sp.). Photo by D. E. Brown.

Plate 27. Southeastern Deciduous and Evergreen Forest (123.1) in the Croatan National Forest in North Carolina. This coastal habitat is dominated by a nearly pure stand of longleaf pine (*Pinus palustrus*). U. S. Forest Service photo taken by Daniel O. Todd in July 1952.

Plate 28. California Evergreen Forest and Woodland (123.2) at ca. 340 m (1100 ft) in the San Jose Hills near Pomoma, Los Angeles County, California. This particular woodland of winter deciduous California walnuts (*Juglans california*) and a few evergreen coast live oaks (*Quercus agrifolia*) is rapidly being urbanized and without protection will soon be destroyed if it has not been so already. The dead branches on the walnut trees are thought to be due to a prolonged drought that began in the winter of 1975 and continued until 1977. Photo by D. E. Brown.

Plate 29. Madrean Evergreen Forest and Woodland (123.3) ca. 1675 m (5500 ft) altitude in the Sierra del Nido, Chihuahua, Mexico. The principal trees at this site are Chihuahua pine (*Pinus leiophylla*), Emory oak or "bellota" (*Quercus emoryi*), and Mexican piñon (*Pinus cembroides*). Photo by D. E. Brown.

Plate 30. Relict Conifer Forest (123.4). In this case a woodland of Monterey cypress (*Cupressus macrocarpa*) on the California seacoast in Monterey County. Without the prevailing sea-breeze from the open ocean these trees would soon succumb to wind-borne disease. U. S. Forest Service photo taken in 1903 by A. Gaskill.

Plate 31. Transvolcanic Evergreen Forest and Woodland (123.5) populated by several species of evergreen oaks (*Quercus* spp.), at least three pines (*Pinus* spp.), and a madroño (*Arbutus* sp.) at ca. 1830 m (6000 ft) altitude on the eastern slopes of the Sierra Nevada de Colima, Jalisco, Mexico. Photo by D. E. Brown.

Plate 32. Guerreran Evergreen Forest and Woodland (123.6) at ca. 1250 m (4100 ft) in the Sierra Madre del Sur, Oaxaca, Mexico. The variety of plants in the woodland is large and includes several short-statured oaks and a juniper as well as genera of more southern derivation. Photo by D. E. Brown.

Plate 33. Guatemalan Cloud Forest (123.7) at 2250 m (7400 ft) altitude near the summit of Sierra de la Tigra, Honduras. Various species of hardwoods, some exceeding 50 m (165 ft) in height, occur in this moisture-laden habitat, which occurs above a forest of *Pinus pseudostrobus*. Resplendent quetzales (*Pharomachrus mocinno*) and black penelopinas (*Penelopina nigra*) are just two of the many interesting birds to be seen and heard in this 7,550 hectare National Park. Photo by D. E. Brown.

Plate 34. Guatemalan Evergreen Forest and Woodland (123.8). A short-statured forest of "ocote" (*Pinus oocarpa*) ca. 1300 m (4300 ft) near Tegucigalpa, Honduras. Where more favorable soils and/or moisture conditions are present, oaks enter the "ocotal" and may become locally dominant. Photo by D. E. Brown.

Plate 35. Veracruz Cloud Forest (123.9) of oaks (*Quercus skinneri* et al.), sweetgum *(Liquidamber styraciflua)*, hickory (*Carya* sp.), and other temperate trees at ca. 1150 m (3775 ft) near Rancho del Cielo in the Sierra de Guatemala on the east slopes of the Sierra Madre Oriental in southern Tamaulipas, Mexico. Note the tank bromeliads and large load of epiphytes on the trees. At slightly higher elevations, a beech *(Fagus mexicana)* enters the forest, which shares numerous genera (e.g., *Acer*, *Prunus*, *Myrica*, and *Carya*) if not species with the Southeastern Deciduous and Evergreen Forest (Martin 1958). This forest is the northernmost home of the singing quail (*Dactylartyx thoracicus*). Photo by D. E. Brown.

Plate 36. San Lucan Evergreen Forest and Woodland (123.1a) atop the Sierra de la Laguna, Baja California Sur, Mexico. The trees present include the endemic "pino pinónero" (*Pinus lagunae*) as well as several endemic oaks, for example, "encino negro" (*Quercus devia*). Photo taken on October 14, 1941, by Edward Ross, San Diego Museum of Natural History.

Plate 37. Alaskan Coastal Scrub (131.1). A thicket of what appears to be Sitka alder (*Alnus sinuata*) on Katmai National Monument, Alaska. U. S. National Park Service photo.

Plate 38. Canadian Subpolar Scrub (131.2) of scrub willows (*Salix* sp.) and willow ptarmigan (*Lagopus lagopus*) near Churchill, Manitoba, Canada. Photo taken in November 1988 by D. E. Brown.

Plate 39. Alaskan Alpine and Subalpine Scrub (131.3) and grizzly bear (*Ursus arctos*) on the slopes of the Cathedral Mountains in Denali National Park and Preserve, Alaska, ca. 1400 m (4600 ft) elevation. Photo by D. E. Brown.

Plate 40. Rocky Mountain Alpine and Subalpine Scrub (131.4). A "krumholtz" of limber pine (*Pinus flexilis*) at an elevation of ca. 2000 m (6560 ft) on the east slope of the Rocky Mountains upslope from The Nature Conservancy's Pine Butte Swamp Reserve adjacent to the Lewis and Clark National Forest in Montana. Photo by D. E. Brown.

Plate 41. Cascade-Sierran Alpine and Subalpine Scrub (131.5) at an altitude of 2530 m (8300 ft) along the Pacific Coast Trail, Nevada County, California. Photo taken by Richard E. Brown in July 1995.

Plate 42. Adirondack-Appalachian Alpine and Subalpine Scrub (131.6) represented here by "Dwarf shrub heath communities" on the slopes of Mount Washington, New Hampshire, ca. 1375 m (4500 ft). The principal species present in these small patches of scrubland are *Vaccinium uliginosum*, *V. vitisidaea*, and *Diapensia lapponica*. Photo by Louella Brown.

Plate 43. Madrean Alpine and Subalpine Scrub (131.7) near the summit of Cerro Potosí, Nuevo Leon, Mexico, ca. 3650 m (12000 ft). Most of the shrubs are a prostrate species of pinyon pine (*Pinus culminicola*), which, as far as is known, is restricted to this mountain. Other subalpine associates include *Juniperus monticola*, *Senecio sanguisorbae*, and *Lupinus cacuminus* (Beaman and Andresen 1966). Although minuscule in extent, this biotic community is the habitat for the endemic salamander *Chiropterotriton priscus*, and perhaps other animals. Photo by D. E. Brown.

Plate 44. Great Basin Montane Scrub (132.1) of *Quercus gambelii* in scrub-form at Raton Pass near the Colorado-New Mexico state line at an altitude of 2350 m (7700 ft). The two conifers present are Rocky Mountain pinyon (*Pinus edulis*) and ponderosa pine (*P. ponderosa*). Photo by D. E. Brown.

Plate 45. Madrean Montane Scrub (132.3) near the summit of the Sierra del Nido, Chihuahua, Mexico. This high-elevation (ca. 2460 m or 8100 ft) but fire-prone "chaparral" of shrubby oaks (*Quercus* sp.) and manzanita (*Arctostaphylos* sp.) is reminiscent of other cold temperate scrublands in the Cascade-Sierran (132.2) and Adirondack-Appalachian (132.4) biogeographic regions. Each of these montane scrublands comes with its own plant and animal components, however, and is biogeographically distinct. Photo by D. E. Brown.

Plate 46. Plains Deciduous Scrub (132.4) of shinnery oak (*Quercus harvardi*) within Plains Grassland at ca. 1130 m (3700 ft) altitude southeast of Roswell, Chaves County, New Mexico. Soil Conservation Service photo taken by Max V. Hodson in 1972.

Plate 47. California Chaparral (133.1) comprised of several evergreen plant species in the San Bernardino National Forest, Riverside County, California, ca. 1220 m (4000 ft) altitude. Photo by C. E. Conrad.

Plate 48. California Coastalscrub (133.2) of California Sagebrush (*Artemisia californica*), sages (*Salvia* spp.), Lemonade-berry (*Rhus integrifolia*), and other shrubs near Dana Point, Orange County, California, altitude ca. 50 m (160 ft). Because of urbanization and other disturbances, these "soft-chaparral" habitats are rapidly shrinking in extent. Photo by D. E. Brown.

Plate 49. Southwestern Interior Chaparral (133.3) containing a shrub live oak (*Quercus turbinella*), desert ceanothus (*Ceanothus greggii*), Fremont mahonia (*Berberis fremontii*), pointleaf manzanita (*Arctostaphhylos pungens*), sacahuista (*Nolina microcarpa*), sugar sumac (*Rhus ovata*), and other shrubs on the Tonto National Forest, Gila County, Arizona, ca. 1600 m (5250 ft). U. S. Forest Service photo taken in 1935.

Plate 50. Chihuahuan Interior Chaparral (133.4) at an altitude of 2150 m (7050 ft) in the Sierra La Leona, Nuevo Leon, Mexico. Present at this location are such characteristic chaparral plants as a shrub live oak (*Quercus cordifolia*?), mountain-mahogany (*Cercocarpus mojadensis*?), ceanothus (*Ceanothus greggi*?), algerita (*Berberis trifoliata*), manzanita (*Arctostaphylos pungens*), cliff-rose (*Cowania plicata*?), and skunkbush (*Rhus trilobta*). All but the last species are evergreen shrubs. A few junipers *(Juniperus mexicanus*?) and yuccas (*Yucca carnerosa*) are also present. Photo by D. E. Brown.

Plate 51. Southeastern Maritime Scrub (133.5) on Jonathan Dickinson State Park north of Jupiter, Florida. These sterile dunes are sparsely clothed in a "chaparral-like" vegetation that here includes turkey oak (*Quercus laevis*) and Chapman oak (*Q. chapmanii*), rosemary (*Ceratiola ericoides*), and an occasional sand pine (*Pinus clausa*). Photo by D. E. Brown.

Plate 52. Alaskan Grassland (141.1) near Eielson Visitor Center, Denali National Park and Preserve, Alaska. The variety of herbaceous plants is large, and the forbs, many possessing showy flowers, greatly outnumber the bunchgrasses. Photo by D. E. Brown.

Plate 53. Rocky Mountain Alpine and Subalpine Grassland (141.2) at ca. 2800 m (9200 ft) on the Apache-Sitgreaves National Forest in Arizona's White Mountains. The most conspicuous grass is Thurber fescue (*Festuca thurberi*). Photo by D. E. Brown.

Plate 54. Cascade-Sierran Alpine and Sub-alpine Grassland (141.3) at an altitude of 2150 m (7050 ft) near Serene Lake, Nevada County, California. It is July, yet the snow-pack has only recently melted, allowing the forbs and grasses to commence their annual growth. Swamp onion (*Allium validum*), ladies tresses (*Spiranthes romanzoffiana*), alum-root (*Heuchera micrantha*), yellow cinquefoil (*Potentilla glandulosa*), meadow hosackia (*Lotus torreyi*), wild hollyhock (Sidalcea reptens), cow parsnip (*Heracleum lanatum*), meadow goldenrod (*Solidago* spp.), sneezeweed (*Helenium bigelovii*), and yellow milfoil (*Achillea millefolium*) are just a few of the many species of flowers likely to be present. Photo taken in 1995 by Richard E. Brown.

Plate 55. Transvolcanic Alpine and Subalpine Grassland (141.6). This is the "zacatonal" habitat of the volcano rabbit (*Romeralagus diazi*). Important "zacaton" grasses include *Muhlenbergia macroura, Festuca rosei, F. amplissima,* and *Stipa ichu* (Fa and Bell 1990). The snow-capped peak in the background is 5452 m (17888 ft) Volcán Popocatépetl southeast of Mexico City. Photo by Alejandro Velázquez.

Plate 56. Plains Grassland (142.1). A southern extension of a "mid-grass" prairie community at an altitude of ca. 1675 m (5500 ft) near El Sueco Junction, Chihuahua, Mexico. The principal species is sideoats grama (*Bouteloua curtipendula*), but *B. gracilis*, *Andropogon gerardii*, *Sporobolus heterolepis*, and *Schizachyrium scoparium* are also present as are numerous forbs. Photo by D. E. Brown.

Plate 57. Great Basin Shrub-Grassland (142.2) dominated by bluebunch wheatgrass (*Agropyron spicatum*) near Kalotus, Franklin County, Washington. Soil Conservation Service photo by Claude C. Dillon.

Plate 58. Oregonian (Pacific Coastal) Grassland (142.3) near Salishaw, Oregon, a "wet-meadow" populated principally by Pacific reedgrass (*Calamagrostis nutkaensis*). Photo by D. E. Brown.

Plate 59. Rocky Mountain Montane Grassland (142.4). A meadow of herbaceous forbs at an altitude of 2590 m (8500 ft) within Rocky Mountain Mountain Conifer Forest on the Apache-Sitgreaves National Forest in Arizona. Here, at the upper elevational limits of this biotic community, the trees are Douglas fir *(Pseudotsuta menziesi)* and white fir (*Abies concolor*). Photo by John N. Theobald.

Plate 60. Cascade-Sierran Montane Grassland (142.5) at an altitude of ca. 2135 m (7000 ft) near La Grulla in the Sierra San Pedro Martir, Baja California Norte, Mexico. Photo taken by E. A. Goldman in July 1905. Although heavily cropped by livestock, these meadow grasslands appear to have remained largely unchanged seventy-five years later.

Plate 61. Chihuahuan (Semidesert) Grassland (143.1) at an altitude of 1465 m (4800 ft) in Sulphur Springs Valley, Cochise County, Arizona. The spiky-appearing shrubs are "palmilla" (*Yucca elata*) and the dominant grass is blue grama (*Bouteloua gracilis*). Such landscapes occupy large tracts of southeastern Arizona, southern New Mexico, southwest Texas, and north-central Mexico. Other Semidesert Grassland communities are more complex, and Semidesert Grassland is an appropriate and convenient designation for a broad spectrum of ecotone and transition communities found between desertscrub and scrubland. Photo by D. E. Brown.

Plate 62. California Valley Grassland (143.2) west of Crow's Landing, Stanislaus County, California, ca. 75 m (250 ft) altitude. The vegetation is almost entirely introduced annual forbs of the genus *Erodium* and such annual alien grasses as *Bromus* and *Avena*. Soil Conservation Service photo taken by M. W. Talbot in 1934.

Plate 63. Gulf Coastal Grassland (143.3) at an altitude of ca. 60 m (200 ft) on Attwater Prairie Chicken National Wildlife Refuge, Colorado County, Texas. The grass cover is both dense and diverse, and includes such characteristic species as Gulf muhly (*Muhlenbergia capillaris*), little bluestem (*Schizachyrium scoparium*), big bluestem (*Andropogon gerardii*), broomsedge bluestem (*A. virginicus*), switchgrass (*Panicum virgatum*), and Indiangrass (*Sorghastrum nutans*). Photo taken in February, 1995, by Jenny Hoskins.

Plate 64. Great Basin Desertscrub (152.1) on the Desert Experimental Range in Utah. The dominant plants are winterfat (*Eurotia lanata*) and shadscale (*Atriplex confertifolia*). U.S. Forest Service photo taken in 1951 by Selar S. Hutchings.

Plate 65. Mohave Desertscrub (153.1) at ca. 1125 m (3700 ft) altitude in Yavapai County, Arizona. Besides such endemic indicators as Joshua-tree (*Yucca brevifolia*) and goldenhead (*Acamptopappus sphaerocephalus*), prevalent plants in this southeastern outlier of the Mohave Desert include creosotebush (*Larrea tridentata*), catclaw acacia (*Acacia greggi*), and beavertail cactus (*Opuntia basilaris*). Photo by D. E. Brown.

Plate 66. Chihuahuan Desertscrub (153.2). This "foothill" or mixed succulent-scrub community at 825 m (2700 ft) altitude on the slopes of the Sierra San Marcos, Coahuila, Mexico, contains a diverse assemblage of plants that include *Yucca macrocarpa, Dasylirion leiophyllum, Agave lecheguilla, Hechtia* spp., *Opuntia leptocaulis, Euphorbia antisyphilitica, Leucophyllum frutescens, Fouquieria splendens, Larrea tridentata,* and *Dyssodia petachaeta.* Photo by D. E. Brown.

Plate 67. Central American Páramo (3,111.1) at an altitude of ca. 3200 m (10500 ft) in the Sierra Talmanaca, Costa Rica. Saint John's wort (*Hypericum* spp.) and dwarf bamboos (*Chusquea* spp.) are among the "chaparral-like" plants that dominate this above-timberline vegetation. Photo by Charlotte M. Christy in July 1994.

Plate 68. Central American Cloud Forest (124.1) at an altitude of 1600 m (5250 ft) on the Monte Verde Reserve in Costa Rica's Cordillera de Tilarán. This 30 to 40 m tall, evergreen forest straddles both the Atlantic and Pacific drainages, and is represented by Nearctic trees belonging to the beech, myrtle, and laurel families as well as such tropical genera as *Ficus*, *Sapium*, and *Cecropia*. Photo by D. E. Brown.

Plate 69. Central American Evergreen Rain Forest (124.2) on the La Selva Biological Reserve, Heredia Province, Costa Rica. Almost 90 percent of this lowland reserve is virgin forest in which the leguminous "Gavilán" (*Pentaclethra macroloba*), and various dwarf palms are important participants. Photo by D. E. Brown.

Plate 70. Central American Semi-Evergreen Forest (124.3) at ca. 300 m (985 ft) altitude on Parque Nacional Santa Rosa, Guanacaste Province, Costa Rica. It is March toward the end of the dry season, and the evergreen trees in the more protected locales stand in marked contrast to their deciduous associates. Photo by D. E. Brown.

Plate 71. Central American Dry Forest (124.4) at Rancho La Pacifica, Guanacaste Province, Costa Rica. The drought-deciduous aspect of the forest is obvious in March 1983. Photo by D. E. Brown.

Plate 72. Campechian Montane Evergreen
Forest (124.5) at an altitude of ca. 400 m
(1300 ft) in the mountains above the Maya
ruins near Palenque in Chiapas, Mexico.
Note the variation in tree trunk forms.
Photo by D. E. Brown.

Plate 73. Campechian Semi-Evergreen Forest (124.6) near Cobá, Quintana Roo, Mexico, in March
1985. Photo by D. E. Brown.

Plate 74. Yucatán Semi-Deciduous Forest (124.7) near Kabáh, Yucatán, Mexico. Note the bromeliad (*Tillandsia recurvata*) growing on the tree branches. Photo taken in March 1993 by D. E. Brown.

Plate 75. Yucatán Dry Deciduous Forest (124.8) near Mayapán, Yucatán, Mexico. Note the scrubby understory and the columnar cacti. Photo by D. E. Brown.

Plate 76. Guerreran Dry Deciduous Forest (124.9) at ca. 1100 m (3600 ft) altitude in the lower Tehuacán Valley near the borders of Oaxaca and Puebla, Mexico. In addition to "pochote" (*Ceiba aesculifolia*), the trees include "copal" and other species of *Bursera*. Photo by D. E. Brown.

Plate 77. Veracruz Evergreen Rain Forest (124.1a) at ca. 100 m (300 ft) altitude near Santa Lucrecia, Veracruz, Mexico. Some of the forest's trees appear to have been cut down, thus favoring the development of a dense secondary forest. Photo taken in January 1904 by E. A. Goldman.

Plate 78. Veracruz Semi-Evergreen Forest (124.1b) at an altitude of ca. 800 m (2625 ft) in the mountains east of Gomez Fariás, Tamaulipas, Mexico. Immediately above this site one encounters Veracruz Cloud Forest. Important if not characteristic trees present at this locality include *Bursera simarubra*, *Cecropia obtusifolia*, and *Brosimum alicastrum*. Photo by D. E. Brown.

Plate 79. Nayarit-Guerreran Semi-Evergreen Forest (124.1c) south of Acaponeta, Nayarit, Mexico. These diverse and beautiful forests are rapidly being converted to agriculture on all but the steepest slopes. Photo by D. E. Brown.

Plate 80. Sinaloan Dry Deciduous Forest (124.1d) during the leafless season in December at ca. 500 m (1640 ft) altitude southeast of Alamos, Sonora, Mexico. The canopy of leguminous trees over-tops the columnar cacti which are mostly hechos (*Pachyereus pecten-aboriginum*). Photo by D. E. Brown.

Plate 81. Tamaulipan Semi-Deciduous Forest (124.1e) at an altitude of ca. 550 m (1800 ft) in the Sierra Tamalare between Ocampo and Tula, Tamaulipas, Mexico. The light-colored plants in the center right of the photograph are flowering soyate (*Dasylirion langissimum*), one of several "indicator species" for this biotic community. Photo by D. E. Brown.

Plate 82. San Lucan Dry Deciduous Forest (124.1f) at its lower limits near La Palmilla in the Cape region of Baja California Sur, Mexico. The white-barked trees are *Lysiloma candida*. Other species present are *Bursera microphylla*, *Karwinsikia humboldtiana*, *Cercidium peninsulare*, *Pithecellobium confine*, and *Pachycereus pringlei*. Photo taken by J. R. Hastings in 1941.

Plate 83. Caribbean Cloud and Montane Evergreen Forest (124.1g) on the slopes of the Sierra Luquillo in the El Yunque Recreation Area of the Caribbean National Forest, Puerto Rico. The presence of tree ferns helps distinguish these higher elevation forests from lower, coastal evergreen forests. Photo by D. E. Brown.

Plate 84. Caribbean Lowland Evergreen Forest (124.1h) on Luquillo Beach, Puerto Rico. Although groves of the widely planted and naturalized coconut palm (*Cocos nucifera*) now almost exclusively dominate many Caribbean beaches, other lowland sites are populated by pines (e.g., *Pinus caribaea*) and/or other evergreen trees. Photo by D. E. Brown.

Plate 85. Caribbean Dry Forest (124.1i) on the southeast coast of the island nation of Dominica. It is January, the rainy season is ending, and trees such as gumbo limbo (*Bursera simaruba*) are beginning to shed their leaves. Photo by D. E. Brown.

Plate 86. Floridian Evergreen (Hammock) Forest (124.1j). A "hammock" community preserved in Red Reef Park within the city of Boca Raton, Florida. Just a few of the tree species present at this site, which is just above sea-level, are gumbo limbo (*Bursera simaruba*), strangler fig (*Ficus aurea*), poisonwood (*Metopium toxiferum*), inkwood (*Exothera paniculata*), leadwood (*Krugiodendron ferreum*), and pigeon plum (*Coccoloba diversifolia*). Most are evergreen and many are restricted to southern Florida and the West Indies. Photo by D. E. Brown.

Plate 87. Guerreran Thornscrub (134.1) in the Rio Atoyac Valley, Puebla, Mexico. Unlike columnar cacti in tropical deciduous forests, the candelabra-like cactus (*Lemaireocereus weberi*) protrudes *above* a diverse scrubland of shrubby trees, bushes, and smaller cacti. Photo by D. E. Brown.

Plate 88. Sinaloan Thornscrub (134.2) in the Sierra Frentón between Rayón and Carbo, Sonora, Mexico, at an altitude of ca. 600 m (1970 ft). The shrubbery is diverse and includes such species as tree-ocotillo (*Fouquieria macdougalii*), hopbush (*Dodonaea viscosa*), *Caesalpinia pumila*, mesquite (*Prosopis juliflora*), organ-pipe cactus (*Stenocerus thurberi*), and a paloverde (*Cercidium microphyllum*). Photo by D. E. Brown.

Plate 89. Tamaulipan Thornscrub (134.3) along the lower Rio Grande between Eagle Pass and Laredo, Texas, ca. 260 m (850 ft) altitude. Included within this landscape are such plants as mesquite (*Prosopis glandulosa*), Texas ranger or "cenizo" (*Leucophyllum frutescens*), several acacias (*Acacia* spp.), and prickly-pear cacti (*Opuntia* spp.). Recently semidesert grassland, this "brush country," called "chaparral" in Texas, is best biogeographically described as thornscrub. Photo by D. E. Brown.

Plate 90. San Lucan Thornscrub (134.4) at ca. 75 m (250 ft) altitude near Cabo San Lucas, Baja California Sur, Mexico. The number of participating plants is large and includes *Jatropha cinerea*, *Bursera microphylla*, *Machaerocereus gummosus*, and *Solanum hindsianum*—all of which are overtopped by *Pachycereus pringlei*. Photo by J. R. Hastings.

Plate 91. Carribbean Thornscrub (134.5) on Buck Island, U. S. Virgin Islands. As on the mainland, the columnar cacti in thornscrub communities overtop the shrubbery. Photo by D. E. Brown.

Plate 92. Central American Thornscrub (134.6) near Comayagua, Honduras. The shrubbery is punctuated by a columnar cactus, a cholla, and an arboreal prickly-pear, as well as numerous small trees. Photo by D. E. Brown.

Plate 93. Central American Savanna Grassland (144.1) on Santa Rosa National Park, Guanacaste Province, Costa Rica. The principal grass is said to be "jaragua" (*Hyparrahenia rufa*), a pasture grass introduced from Africa. The debate over whether Central American savannas are "natural" or "maintained" is now largely moot given the widespread and frequent occurrence of both natural and man-induced fires in this type of vegetation. Photo by D. E. Brown.

Plate 94. Guerreran Savanna Grassland (144.2) off Mexican Highway 190 near Huajuapan de León, Oaxaca, Mexico. The trees are mostly the sombrero palm (*Brahea dulcis*) with some "nance" (*Byrsonima crassifolia*) and "raspaviejo" (*Curatella americana*) present. The grasses include both Nearctic and Neotropical genera, e.g., *Bouteloua* and *Cynodon*. Photo by D. E. Brown.

Plate 95. Campechian-Veracruz Savanna Grassland (144.3) near the Campeche-Tabasco border in Mexico. The factors determining the presence of savanna vegetation in the tropics are complex and involve soil moisture and composition, seasonal drought, landscape physiognomy, fire frequency, and human history (Borhidi 1991). Photo by D. E. Brown.

Plate 96. Caribbean Savanna Grassland (144.4) in Mayaguez District, Puerto Rico. The trees are mesquites (*Prosopis* sp.). Tropical grasslands or savannas can be found in all Neotropical biotic provinces, each having its own peculiarities and constituents. Photo by D. E. Brown.

Plate 97. Sonoran Savanna Grassland (144.5) at 610 m (2000 ft) altitude south of Benjamin Hill, Sonora, Mexico. The principal grasses are Rothrock grama (*Bouteloua rothrockii*) and threeawns (*Aristida* spp.); the trees are mesquite (*Prosopis velutina*), paloverdes *(Cercidium microphyllum, C. floridum)*, and ironwood (*Olnea tesota*). The shrub in the immediate center is a young acacia (*Acacia angustissima*). This area has since been increasingly invaded by scrub. Photo taken by Roy E. Tomlinson in the summer of 1968.

106

Plate 98. Tamaulipan Savanna Grassland (144.6) just northeast of the Calles railroad station in Tamaulipas, Mexico, ca. 400 m (1300 ft). The principal grass is a species of *Cynodon* which occurs with several genera of both tropical and temperate origin. Photo by D. E. Brown.

Plate 99. Sonoran Desertscrub (154.1). This and the following figure show two extreme views. This photograph was taken in the foothills of the Sierra de los Mochos in Sonora, Mexico, at an altitude of ca. 300 m (985 ft). Four species of columnar cacti (*Pachycereus pringlei, Stenocereus thurberi, Lophocereus schotii,* and *Carnegia gigantea*) are visible in this landscape. About the only species common to both localities is blue paloverde (*Cercidium floridum*). Photo by D. E. Brown.

Plate 100. Sonoran Desertscrub (154.1). This photograph was taken in the dunefields near Glamis, California, at an altitude of ca. 50 m (160 ft). See plate 99 for contrast. Photo by D. E. Brown.

Plate 101. Arctic Wet Tundra (211.). It is springtime in this Alaskan Wet Tundra biotic community within Alaska's Colville River Delta, the ground and ponds above the permafrost have thawed, and the marsh marigold (*Coetha palustrus*) is in bloom. U. S. Fish and Wildlife Service photo taken by Urban C. Nelson.

Plate 102. Boreal Swamp and Riparian Forest (221.). Both Canadian Swamp Forest and Canadian Swamp Scrub biotic communities are represented in this U.S. Fish and Wildlife Service photo taken by Charles D. Evans east of Bearhead Lake in Manitoba, Canada. The dark trees are primarily black spruce (*Picea mariana*) accompanied by willows (*Salix* sp.) and alders (*Alnus* sp.).

Plate 103. Cold Temperate Swamp and Riparian Forest (222.). This particular Northeastern Riparian Forest along the Des Moines River Valley in Iowa is composed largely of Eastern cottonwood (*Populus deltoides*) and silver maple (*Acer saccharinum*). U.S. Forest Service photo taken in July 1945 by A. L. McComb.

Plate 104. Warm Temperate Swamp and Riparian Forest (223.). Baldcypress (*Taxodium distichum*) almost exclusively occupies this Southeastern Swamp Forest in North Carolina. U.S. Forest Service photo taken by W. H. Shaffer in May 1940.

Plate 105. Arctic-Boreal Swamp Scrub (231.). A small area of Rocky Mountain Subalpine Swamp Scrub above 2600 m (8500 ft) within the Phelps Botanical Area of the Apache-Sitgreaves National Forest in Arizona. The shrubbery appears to be composed chiefly of Bebb willow (*Salix bebbiana*) and red-osier dogwood (*Cornus stolonifera*) with some thin-leaf alder (*Alnus tenuifolia*) also present. Photo taken by Rex King in September 1945.

Plate 106. Cold Temperate Swamp and Riparian Scrub (232.). Willows (*Salix* spp.) are the princi-pal plants making up this Rocky Mountain Riparian Scrub along the headwaters of the Snake River in Teton County, Wyoming. Note the sedge meadow (Rocky Mountain Marshland) in the center of the photo and the island of Rocky Mountain Swamp Forest. Photo by D. E. Brown.

Plate 107. Warm Temperate Swamp and Riparian Scrub (233.). A California Maritime Swamp Scrub of pickleweed (*Salicornia virginica*) and other halophytes in southern San Francisco Bay, Santa Clara County, California. Photo by D. E. Brown.

Plate 108. Arctic-Boreal Marshland (241.). A tiny sedge-populated *cienéga* of Rocky Mountain Subalpine Marshland located at 2740 m (9000 ft) atop the Pinaleño Mountains, Graham County, Arizona. Photo by D. E. Brown.

Plate 109. Cold Temperate Marshland (242.). A Great Basin Marshland located at Ruby Lake, Elko County, Nevada. The principal marsh emergents are roundstem bulrush (*Scirpus acutus*) and cattail (*Typha latifolia*). Photo by D. E. Brown.

Plate 110. Warm Temperate Marshland (243.). This U.S. Fish and Wildlife Service photograph by George C. Moore of the mouth of the Satilla River in Georgia shows a Southeastern Maritime Marshland of needlegrass (*Juncus roemerianus*).

Plate 111. Arctic-Boreal Strand (251.) of bare gravel and melted ice left by a receding glacier in Olympic National Park, Washington. U.S. National Park Service photo by George A. Grant.

Plate 112. Cold Temperate Strand (252.). A U.S. Park Service photo of Oregonian Maritime Strand taken in February 1961 by Louis G. Kirk at Rialto Beach, Olympic National Park, Washington.

Plate 113. Warm Temperate Strand (253.) represented by California Maritime Strand at Scammon's Lagoon, Baja California Norte, Mexico. This sparsely vegetated community on a mud substrate, although a true wetland, is reminiscent of, and analogous to, the desertland formation of upland vegetation. A stand of cordgrass (*Spartina* sp.) forms a marshland in the background. Photo by D. E. Brown.

Plate 114. Tropical-Subtropical Swamp, Riparian, and Oasis Forest and Woodland (3,224.). This and the following figure illustrate the diversity of these biotic communities. This photograph shows a Yucatán Maritime Swamp Forest of mangroves (mostly *Rhizophora mangle*) near Celustún, Yucatán, Mexico. Photo by D. E. Brown.

Plate 115. Tropical-Subtropical Swamp, Riparian, and Oasis Forest and Woodland (3,224.). This photograph illustrates a Sonoran Riparian Forest of California fan palms (*Washingtonia filifera*) within the Sonoran Desert near Wickenburg, Arizona. Photo by D. E. Brown. See also plate 114.

Plate 116. Tropical-Subtropical Swamp and Riparian Scrub (234.). A Sonoran Swamp Scrub of the adventive saltcedar (*Tamarix parviflora*) in the delta of the Colorado River in Baja California Norte, Mexico. Photo by D. E. Brown.

Plate 117. Tropical-Subtropical Marshland (244.). A Caribbean Interior Marshland (foreground) surrounds an *etang* or pond within Evergreen Forest on Guadeloupe Island's spacious Parc Naturel. Photo by D. E. Brown.

Plate 118. Tropical-Subtropical Strand (254.). A riparian community of Sonoran Interior Strand in the San Pedro River bed within the Sonoran Desert in southern Arizona. Photo by D. E. Brown.

Literature Cited

Agassiz, L. 1854. Sketch of the natural provinces of the animal world and their relation to the different types of man. In J. C. Nott and G. R. Gliddon. Types of mankind. Lippincott, Grambo and Company, Philadelphia.

Aldrich, J. W. 1967. Biomes of North America. Map. In The wild turkey and its management, O. H. Hewitt, ed. Wildlife Society, Washington, D.C.

Allen, J. A. 1878. The geographic distribution of mammals. Bulletin, U.S. Geological and Geographical Survey of the Territories 4:39–343.

————. 1892. The geographic distribution of North American mammals. Bulletin of the American Museum of Natural History 4:199–242.

————. 1893. The geographical origin and distribution of North American birds, considered in relation to faunal areas of North America. Auk 10:97–150.

Allen, T. F. H., and T. W. Hoekstra. 1992. Toward a unified ecology. Columbia University Press, New York.

Allred, D. M., D. E. Beck, and C. D. Jorgensen. 1963. Biotic communities of the Nevada Test Site. Brigham Young University Science Bulletin 2(2).

Anderson, J. R., E. E. Hardy, and J. T. Roach. 1972. A land use classification system for use with remote sensor data. United States Geological Survey Circular 671:1–15.

Anderson, J. R., E. E. Hardy, J. T. Roach, and R. E. Witmer. 1976. A land use and land cover classification system for use with remote sensor data. U.S. Geological Survey Professional Paper 964.

Arriaga, L., and A. Ortega, eds. 1988. La Sierra de la Laguna de Baja California Sur. Centro de Investigaciones Biológicas de Baja California Sur, La Paz, Baja California Sur, A. C. Publicación No. 1.

Avers, P. E., D. T. Cleland, W. H. McNab, M. E. Jensen, R. G. Bailey, T. King, C. B. Goudey, and W. E. Russell. 1993. National hierarchical framework of ecological units. ECOMAP, U.S. Department of Agriculture, Forest Service, Washington, D.C.

Bailey, R. G. 1976. Ecoregions of the United States. U.S. Department of Agriculture, Forest Service, Washington, D.C. Map (scale 1:7,500,000).

————. 1989a. Ecoregions of the continents. U.S. Department of Agriculture, Forest Service, Washington, D.C. Elsevier Sequoia S.A. Lausanne, Switzerland, for the Foundation for Environmental Conservation. Map (scale 1:30,000,000).

————. 1989b. Explanatory supplement to ecoregions map of the continents. Environmental Conservation 16(4):307–9.

Bailey, R. G., and C. T. Cushwa. 1981. Ecoregions of North America, after the classification of J.M. Crowley. U.S. Department of the Interior, Fish and Wildlife Service, Office of Biological Services, Eastern Energy and Land Use Team, Washington, D.C. The Survey, Reston, Virginia. Map (scale 1:12,000,000).

Barbour, M. G., and W. D. Billings, eds. 1988. North American terrestrial vegetation. Cambridge University Press, Cambridge.

Barbour, M. G., and J. Major, eds. 1977. Terrestrial vegetation of California. Second edition, revised. California Native Plant Society Special Publication 9.

Beaman, J. H., and J. W. Andresen. 1966. The vegetation, floristics and phytogeography of the summit of Cerro Potosí, Mexico. American Midland Naturalist 75:1–33.

Beard, J. S. 1953. Savannah vegetation of northern tropical America. Ecological Monographs 23:149–215.

Betancourt, J. L., T. R. Van Devender, and P. S. Martin. 1990. Packrat middens: the last 40,000 years of biotic change. University of Arizona Press, Tucson.

Billings, W. D. 1973. Tundra grasslands, herblands and shrublands and the role of herbivores. In Grasslands Ecology: A Symposium, R. H. Kesel, ed. School of Geoscience, Louisiana State University, Baton Rouge.

Billings, W. D., and H. A. Mooney. 1968. The ecology of arctic and alpine plants. Biological Review 43:481–529.

Blair, W. F. 1950. The biotic provinces of Texas. Texas Journal of Science 2:93–117.

Bliss, L. C. 1988. Arctic tundra and polar desert biome. In North American terrestrial vegetation, M. G. Barbour and W. D. Billings, eds., 1–32. Cambridge University Press, Cambridge.

Borhidi, A. 1991. Phytogeography and vegetation ecology of Cuba (includes a map, scale 1:250,000, by A. Borhidi and O. Muñiz). Akadémiai Kiadó, Budapest, Hungary.

Bourgeron, P. S., L. D. Engelking, H. C. Humphries, E. Muldavin, and W. H. Moir. 1995. Assessing the conservation value of the Gray Ranch: rarity, diversity, and representativeness. Desert Plants 11(2–3):1–68.

Braun, E. L. 1950. Deciduous forests of eastern North America. Blakiston Company, Incorporated, Philadelphia, Pennsylvania. (Reprinted in 1964 by Hafner Publishing Company, New York.)

Braun-Blanquet, J. 1932. Plant sociology: the study of plant communities. (Translated by G. D. Fuller and H.S. Conrad.) McGraw-Hill Book Company, Incorporated, New York.

Breceda, A., J. L. Leon, L. R. Coria, and L. Arriaga. 1994. The tropical dry forest of the Sierra de la Laguna: a phytogeographical analysis. Conference on Biodiversity and Management of the Madrean Achipelago: the sky islands of southwestern United States and northwestern Mexico: September 19–23, 1994, Tucson, Arizona. Abstracts: 90–91.

Brown, D. E. 1973. The natural vegetative communities of Arizona. Arizona Resources Information System, Phoenix. Map (scale 1:500,000).

———. 1980. A system for classifying cultivated and cultured lands within a systematic classification of natural ecosystems. Journal of the Arizona-Nevada Academy of Science 15:48–53.

———, ed. 1982. The biotic communities of the American Southwest— United States and Mexico. Desert Plants 4(1–4):1–341. Reprinted with revisions in 1994 by University of Utah Press, Salt Lake City, Utah.

Brown, D. E., and C. H. Lowe. 1974a. A digitized computer-compatible classification for natural and potential vegetation in the Southwest with particular reference to Arizona. Journal of the Arizona Academy of Science (Supplement 2):1–11.

———. 1974b. The Arizona system for natural and potential vegetation— illustrated summary through the fifth digit for the North American

Southwest. Journal of the Arizona Academy of Science 9 (Supplement 3):1–56.

————. 1980, 1994. Biotic communities of the Southwest. U.S. Department of Agriculture, Forest Service General Technical Report, RM-78. Rocky Mountain Forest and Range Experiment Station, Fort Collins, Colorado. Map (scale 1:1,000,000). Reprinted in 1994 by University of Utah Press.

Brown, D. E., C. H. Lowe, and C. P. Pase. 1979. A digitized classification system for the biotic communities of North America, with community (series) and association examples for the Southwest. Journal of the Arizona-Nevada Academy of Science 14 (Supplement 1):1–16. Reprinted as an appendix in Biotic Communities of the Southwest: United States and Mexico, D. E. Brown, ed. 1982. Desert Plants 4(1–4):1–341.

————. 1980. A digitized systematic classification for ecosystems with an illustrated summary of the natural vegetation of North America. U.S. Department of Agriculture, Forest Service General Technical Report, RM-73. Rocky Mountain Forest and Range Experiment Station, Fort Collins, Colorado.

Bruner, W. E. 1931. The vegetation of Oklahoma. Ecological Monographs 1:99–188.

Carnahan, J. A. 1976. Natural vegetation. Atlas of Australian Resources, Canberra. Vol. 2:1–26 and Map (scale 1:6,000,000).

Carr, A. F. 1950. Outline of a classification of animal habitats in Honduras. Bulletin of the American Museum of Natural History 94:563–94.

Chapman, D. M., ed. 1993. Canada vegetation cover, 1:7,500,000. Map MCR4182. Canada Map Office, Energy, Mines and Resources, Information Canada, Ottawa.

Christensen, N.L. 1988. Vegetation of the southeastern Coastal Plain. In North American terrestrial vegetation, M.G. Barbour and W.D. Billings, eds. Cambridge University Press, Cambridge.

Clements, F. E. 1916. Plant succession: an analysis of the development of vegetation. Carnegie Institution of Washington (Publication 242), Washington, D.C.

————. 1920. Plant indicators: the relation of plant communities to process and practice. Carnegie Institution of Washington (Publication 290), Washington, D.C.

Clements, F. E., and V. E. Shelford. 1939. Bio-ecology. John Wiley and Sons, New York.

Cooper, J. G. 1859. On the distribution of the forests and trees of North America, with notes on its physical geography. Smithsonian Institution Annual Report to the Board of Regents:246–80.

Cowardin, L. M., V. Carter, F. C. Golet, and E. T. La Roe. 1979. Classification of wetlands and deep water habitats of the United States. U.S. Department of the Interior, Fish and Wildlife Service, Office of Biological Services, Washington D.C. FWS/OBS-79/31.

Cowles, H. C. 1908. An ecological aspect of the conception of species. American Naturalist 42:265–71.

Cox, C. B., I. N. Healey, and P. D. Moore. 1976. Biogeography: an ecological and evolutionary approach. Second Edition. Blackwell Science Publications, Oxford.

Crowley, J. M. 1967. Biogeography in Canada. Canadian Geographic 11:312–26.

Dansereau, P. M. 1957. Biogeography; an ecological perspective. Ronald Press Company, New York.

Darlington, P. J., Jr. 1957. Zoogeography: the geographical distribution of animals. John Wiley and Sons, Incorporated, New York.

Daubenmire, R. F. 1938. Merriam's life zones of North America. Quarterly Review of Biology 13:327–32.

———. 1946. The life zone problem in the north intermountain region. Northwest Science 20:28–38.

Daubenmire, R. F., and J. Daubenmire. 1968. Forest vegetation of eastern Washington and northern Idaho. Washington Agriculture Experiment Station Technical Bulletin 60.

DeLaubenfels, D. J. 1975. Mapping the world's vegetation. Syracuse University Press, Geographical Series 4, Syracuse, New York.

Demarchi, D. A. 1993. An introduction to the ecoregions of British Columbia. Third Edition. (Includes a map, scale 1:2,000,000.) Ministry of the Environment, Lands and Parks, Victoria.

Dice, L. R. 1923. Life zones and mammalian distribution. Journal of Mammalogy 4:39–47.

———. 1943. The biotic provinces of North America. University of Michigan Press, Ann Arbor.

Dick-Peddie, W. A., and W. H. Moir. 1970. Vegetation of the Organ Mountains, New Mexico. Colorado State University, Range Science Department Science Series 4. Fort Collins, Colorado.

Dokuchaev, V. V. 1987. Classification and diagnostics of soils of the USSR. Russian Translation Series 42. A. A. Balkema, Rotterdam.

Driscoll, R. S., D. L. Merkel, D. L. Radloff, D. E. Snyder, and J. S. Hagihara. 1984. An ecological land classification framework for the United States. U.S. Department of Agriculture, Forest Service Miscellaneous Publication No. 1439.

Drüde, O. 1887. Atlas der pflanzenverbreitung. Berghaus' Physik Atlas V. Gotha:1–6.

Dyksterhuis, E. J. 1957. The savannah concept and its use. Ecology 38:435–42.

Eidenshink, J. C. 1992. The 1990 conterminous U.S. AVHRR data set. Photogrammetric Engineering and Remote Sensing 58(6):809–13.

Engler, A. 1879–1882. Versuch einer entwicklungsgeschichte der planzen-welt, insbesondere der florengebrete seit der tertiarperiode. 2 volumes. Engelmann, Leipzig.

Fa, J. E., and D. J. Bell. 1990. The volcano rabbit Romerolagus diazi. In Rabbits, hares and pikas, J. A. Chapman and J. E. C. Flux, eds., 143–46. 1990. International Union for Conservation of Nature and Natural Resources, Gland, Switzerland.

Fleming, T. H. 1973. Numbers of mammal species in North and Central American forest communities. Ecology 54:555–63.

Flores Mata, G., J. Jiminéz Lopez, X. Madrigal Sanchez, F. Moncayo Ruiz, and F. Takaki. 1971. Memoria del mapa de tipos de vegetación de la República Mexicana. Secretaria de Recursos Hidráulicos, Subsecretaria de Planeación, Dirección General de Estudios, Dirección de Agrologia, Mexico, D.F. (Manual, and Map, scale 1:2,000,000.)

Franklin, J. F. 1977. The biosphere reserve program in the United States. Science 195:262–67.

Franklin, J. F., and C. T. Dyrness. 1973. Natural vegetation of Oregon and Washington. U.S. Department of Agriculture, Forest Service General Technical Report PNW–8. Pacific Northwest Forest and Range Experiment Station, Portland, Oregon.

Frye, R. G., K. L. Brown, and C. A. McMahan. 1984. The vegetation types of Texas. Texas Parks and Wildlife Department, Austin. Map (scale 1:500,000).

Garrison, G. A., A. J. Bjugstad, D. A. Duncan, M. E. Lewis, and D. R. Smith. 1977. Vegetation and environmental features of forest and range ecosystems. U.S. Department of Agriculture, Forest Service (Agricultural Handbook 475). Washington, D.C.

Gaussen, H. 1953. A proposed ecological vegetation map. Surveying and Mapping 13:168–73.

Gentry, H. S. 1942. Rio Mayo plants; a study of the flora and vegetation of the valley of the Rio Mayo, Sonora. Carnegie Institution of Washington (Publication 527).

———. 1982. Sinaloan deciduous forest. In Biotic communities of the Southwest—United States and Mexico, D. E. Brown, ed., 73–77. 1982. Desert Plants 4(1–4):1–342. (Reprinted with revisions in 1994. University of Utah Press, Salt Lake City, Utah.)

Gill, T. 1885. The principles of zoography. Proceedings of the Biological Society of Washington 2:1–39.

Gleason, H. A. 1926. The individualistic concept of the plant association. Torrey Botanical Club Bulletin 53:7–26. (Reprinted in 1939 in American Midland Naturalist 21:92–110.)

Goldman, E. A. 1920. Mammals of Panama. Smithsonian Miscellaneous Collections 69(4).

Goldman, E. A., and R. T. Moore. 1945. The biotic provinces of Mexico. Journal of Mammalogy 26:347–60.

Good, R. D. 1964. The geography of the flowering plants. Third edition. Longman's, London.

Graham, R. W., E. L. Lundelius, Jr., M. A. Graham, E. K. Schroeder, R. S. Toomey III, E. Anderson, A. D. Barnosky, J. A. Burns, C. S. Churcher, D. K. Grayson, R. D. Guthrie, C. R. Harington, G. T. Jefferson, L. D. Martin, H. G. McDonald, R. E. Morlan, H. A. Semkin, Jr., S. D. Webb, L. Werdelin, and M. C. Wilson. 1996. Spatial response of mammals to late quaternary environmental fluctuations. Science 272:1601–6.

Greller, A. M. 1988. Deciduous Forest. In North American terrestrial vegetation, M. G. Barbour and W. D. Billings, eds., 287–316. 1988. Cambridge University Press, Cambridge.

Hall, E. R. 1946. Mammals of Nevada. University of California Press, Berkeley.

Hall E. R., H. Monroe, and J. Grinnell. 1919. Life zone indicators in California. Proceedings of the California Academy of Sciences. 4th Series 9:37–67.

Halliday, W. E. D. 1937. A forest classification for Canada. Canada Department of Mines and Resources, Forest Service Bulletin 89.

Harshberger, J. W. 1911. Phytogeographic survey of North America. G. E. Stechert, New York.

Hayden, B. P., G. C. Ray, and R. Dolan. 1984. Classification of coastal and marine environments. Environmental Conservation 11:199–207.

Hayward, C. L. 1948. Biotic communities of the Wasatch chaparral, Utah. Ecological Monographs 18:473–506.

Hesse, R., W. C. Allee, and K. P. Schmidt. 1937. Ecological animal geography. John Wiley and Sons, Incorporated, New York.

Holdridge, L. R. 1959. Mapa ecologico de Central America. Según publicaciones de Unidad de Recursos Naturalos, Departmento de Asuntos Económicos, Unión Panamericana.

———. 1967. Life zone ecology. Revised edition; with photographic supplement prepared by Joseph A. Tosi, Jr. Tropical Science Center, San Jose, Costa Rica.

———. 1969. Diagroma para la clasificación de zonas de vida o formaciones vegetales del mundo. In República de Costa Rica, mapa ecológico (scale 1: 750,000), J. A. Tosi, Jr. 1969. Centro Cientfico Tropical, San Jose, Costa Rica.

Holling, C. S. 1995. What barriers? What bridges? In Barriers and bridges to the renewal of ecosystems and institutions, L. H. Gunderson, C. S. Holling, and S. S. Light, eds., 3–34. Columbia University Press, New York.

Humboldt, A. von. 1817. De distributione geographica plantarum. Paris.

Humboldt, A. von, and A. Bonpland. 1807. Ideen zu einer geographie der pflanzen nebst einem naturgemalde der tropenlander. Cotta, Tubingen; Neudruck Geest, and Portig, Leipzig (1960).

Huxley, T. H. 1868. On the classification and distribution of the Alectoromorphae and Heteromorphae. Proceedings of the London Zoological Society, 294–319.

IUCN (International Union for Conservation of Nature and Natural Resources). 1974. Biotic provinces of the world—further development of a system for defining and classifying natural regions for purposes of conservation. Prepared by the Secretariat of IUCN as a contribution to Unesco's Man and the Biosphere Programme, Project Number 8. IUCN Occasional Paper 9. IUCN, Morges, Switzerland.

———. 1992. Protected areas of the world: a review of national systems. Compiled by the World Conservation Monitoring Centre, in collabo-ration with the IUCN Commission on National Parks and Protected Areas for the Fourth World Congress on National Parks and Protected Areas, Caracas, Venezuela, 10–21 February 1992. International Union for Conservation of Nature and Natural Resources (IUCN), Gland, Switzerland. 4 volumes.

Jennings, M. 1988. Use of the Holdridge life zone system: an annotated bibliography. Vance Bibliography and Publication Administration series—bibliography. Series Number P2320. Vance Bibliographies, Monticello, Illinois.

Jensen, H. A. 1947. A system for classifying vegetation in California. California Fish and Game 33:199–266.

Kendeigh, S. C. 1932. A study of Merriam's temperature laws. The Wilson Bulletin 44:129–43.

———. 1952. History and evaluation of various concepts of plant and animal communities in North America. In Selections from the litera-ture of American biogeography, K.B. Sterling. ed. 1974. Arno Press, New York.

Kiester, A. R. 1971. Species density of North American amphibians and reptiles. Systematic Zoology 20:127–37.

Klopfer, P. H., and R. H. MacArthur. 1960. Niche size and faunal diver-sity. American Naturalist 94:293–300.

Köppen, W. 1931. Gundriss der Klimakunde. Walter de Gruyter Co., Berlin, Germany.

Küchler, A. W. 1947. A geographic system of vegetation. Geographical Review 37:233–40.

———. 1964. The potential natural vegetation of the conterminous United States. American Geographical Society of New York, Special Publica-tion; Number 36. Map (scale 1,7,000,000) accompanied by manual.

———. 1977. Natural vegetation of California. Map (scale 1:1,000,000). In Terrestrial vegetation of California, M. G. Barbour and J. Major, eds. Second edition, revised. California Native Plant Society Special Publication 9.

Layser, E. F. 1974. Vegetative classification: its application to forestry in the northern Rocky Mountains. Journal of Forestry 2:354–57.

Leopold, A. S. 1959. Wildlife of New Mexico. University of California Press, Berkeley.

Linnaeus, C. 1758. Systema naturae. Tenth edition. Laurentii Salvii, Stockholm.

Livingston, B. E., and F. Shreve. 1921. The distribution of vegetation in the United States, as related to climatic conditions. Carnegie Institution of Washington (Publication Number 284).

Loveland, T. R., J. W. Merchant, D. O. Ohlen, and J. F. Brown. 1991. Development of a land-cover characteristics database for the conterminous U.S. Photogrammetric Engineering and Remote Sensing 57:1453–63.

Lowe, C. H., Jr. 1964. Arizona's natural environment: landscapes and habitats. University of Arizona Press, Tucson.

MacKinnon, A., D. Meidinger, and K. Klinka. 1992. Use of the biogeoclimatic ecosystem classification system in British Columbia. Forestry Chronicle 68:100–120.

MacMahon, J. A. 1988. Warm deserts. In North American terrestrial vegetation, M. G. Barbour and W. D. Billings, eds., 231–64. 1988. Cambridge University Press, Cambridge.

MacMahon, J. A., and T. F. Wieboldt. 1983. Applying biogeographic principles to resource management: a case study evaluating Holdridge's life zone model. Great Basin Naturalist Memoirs 2:245–57.

Martin, A. C., N. Hotchkiss, F. M. Uhler, and W. S. Bourn. 1953. Classification of wetlands of the United States. U.S. Department of the Interior, Fish and Wildlife Service, Special Scientific Report—Wildlife 20:1–14.

Martin, P. S. 1958. A biogeography of reptiles and amphibians in the Gómes Fariás region, Tamaulipas, Mexico. Museum of Zoology, University of Michigan, Ann Arbor, Miscellaneous Publications, Number 101.

Matvejev, S. 1961. Biogeography of Yugoslavia. Biol. Instit. Monogr. 9:1–9. Belgrade.

Maxwell, J. R., C. Deacon-Williams, C. J. Edwards, M. E. Jensen, H. Parrott, S. J. Paustian, and K. Stein. 1994. Draft hierarchical framework of aquatic ecological units in North America. ECOMAP, U.S. Department of Agriculture, Forest Service.

Maycock, P. F. 1979. A preliminary survey of the vegetation of Ontario as a basis for the establishment of a comprehensive Nature Reserve system. Provencial Parks Branch, Ontario Ministry of Natural Resources, Toronto, Ontario.

McAuliffe, J. R. 1995. Landscape evolution, soil formation and Arizona's desert grasslands. In The desert grassland, M. P. McClaran and T. R. Van Devender, eds., 100–129. University of Arizona Press, Tucson.

McClaran, M. P., and T. R. Van Devender, eds. 1995. The desert grassland. University of Arizona Press, Tucson.

McIntosh, R. P. 1985. The background of ecology: concept and theory. Cambridge University Press, Cambridge.

McLachlan, G. R., and R. Liversidge. 1962. Biotic provinces of southern Africa. In Distribution of birds in relation to vegetation, R. Liversidge. Annals of the Cape Provincial Museum 2:143–51.

McNeely, J. A., and K. R. Miller. 1983. IUCN National Parks and protected areas: priorities for action. Environmental Conservation 10:13–21.

Meidinger, D., and J. Pojar, eds. 1991. Ecosystems of British Columbia. British Columbia Ministry of Forests, Research Branch, Victoria.

Merriam, C. H. 1892. The geographic distribution of life in North America with special reference to the Mammalia. Annual Presidential Address to U.S. Biological Survey 12:365–415 (also 1891. Annual Report of the Board of Regents of the Smithsonian Institution, Washington D.C.).

———. 1894a. Laws of temperature control of the geographic distribution of terrestrial animals and plants. National Geographic Magazine 6:229–38.

———. 1894b. The geographic distribution of animals and plants in North America. Yearbook of the United States Department of Agriculture, Washington, D.C.

———. 1898. Life-zones and crop-zones of the United States. United States Department of Agriculture, Division of Biological Survey, Bulletin 10.

———. 1903. Plan for a biological survey of South and Central America. Carnegie Institution of Washington Yearbook 1:267–69.

Merriam, C. H., and L. Stejneger. 1890. Results of a biological survey of the San Francisco Mountain region and desert of the Little Colorado in Arizona. North American Fauna 3.

Merriam, C. H., V. Bailey, E. W. Nelson, and E. A. Preble. 1910. Zone map of North America. U.S. Department of Agriculture, Biological Survey, Washington D.C.

Miller, A. H. 1951. An analysis of the distribution of the birds of California. University of California Publications in Zoology 50(6):531–644.

Morafka, D. J. 1977. A biogeographical analysis of the Chihuahuan Desert through its herpetofauna. Junk, The Hague.

Mueller-Dombois, D., and H. Ellenberg. 1974. Aims and methods of vegetation ecology. John Wiley and Sons, New York.

Muller, C. H. 1947. Vegetation and climate of Coahuila, Mexico. Madroño 9:33–57.

Munz, P. A., and D. D. Keck. 1949. California plant communities. El Aliso 2:87–105.

———. 1950. California plant communities—supplement. El Aliso 2:199–202.

Murie, O. J. 1959. Fauna of the Aleutian Islands, Alaska Peninsula. U.S. Department of the Interior, Fish and Wildlife Service, North American Fauna 61.

Nature Conservancy, The. 1994a. Standardized national vegetation classification system. National Biological Survey/National Park Service Vegetation Mapping Program. 81-page mimeo plus appendix on a national list of "alliances."

———. 1994b. Field methods for vegetation mapping. National Biological Survey/ National Park Service Vegetation Mapping Program.

Nature Conservancy, The, Community Ecology Group, Southeast Regional Office. 1997. International classification of ecological communities: terrestrial vegetation of the southeastern United States. Review copy. The Nature Conservancy Southeast Regional Office and the Southern Conservation Science Department, Chapel Hill, North Carolina.

Neuhäusl, R. 1990. Unified classification of European natural forests: the approach of the vegetation map of Europe. Vegetatio 89:173–81.

Odum, E. P. 1945. The concept of the biome as applied to the distribution of North American birds. Wilson Bulletin 57:191–201.

Omernik, J. M. 1987. Ecoregions of the conterminous United States. Supplement to the Annals of the Association of American Geographers 77(1):118–25. Map (scale 1:7,500,000).

Oosting, H. J. 1956. The study of plant communities; an introduction to plant ecology. Second edition. W. H. Freeman, San Francisco.

Patton, D. R. 1978. RUNWILD: A storage and retrieval system for wildlife habitat information. U.S. Department of Agriculture, Forest Service, Rocky Mountain Forest and Range Experiment Station, Fort Collins, Colorado. General Technical Report RM-51.

Pearson, D. L. 1994. Selecting indicator taxa for the quantitative assessment of biodiversity. Philosophical Transactions of the Royal Society of London B 345:75–79.

Pearson, D. L., and F. Cassola. 1992. World-wide species richness patterns of tiger beetles (Coleoptera: Cicindelidae): indicator taxon for biodiversity and conservation studies. Conservation Biology 6:376–91.

Peet, R. K. 1988. Forests of the Rocky Mountains. In North American terrestrial vegetation, M. G. Barbour and W. D. Billings, eds., 64–101. Cambridge University Press, Cambridge.

Pfister, R. D., B. L. Kovalchik, S. F. Arno, and R. C. Presby. 1977. Forest habitat types of Montana. U.S. Department of Agriculture, Forest Service, Intermountain Forest and Range Experiment Station, Ogden, Utah. General Technical Report INT-34.

Pitelka, F. A. 1941. Distribution of birds in relation to major biotic communities. American Midland Naturalist 25:113–37.

Pojar, J., K. Klinka, and D. V. Meidinger. 1987. Biogeoclimatic classification in British Columbia. Forest Ecology and Management 22:119–54.

Ramamoorthy, T. P., R. Bye, A. Lot, and J. Fa, eds. 1993. Biological diversity of Mexico: origins and distributions. Oxford University Press, New York.

Rasmussen, D. I. 1941. Biotic communities of the Kaibab Plateau, Arizona. Ecological Monographs 11:229–75.

Ray, G. C. 1975. A preliminary classification of coastal and marine environments. International Union for Conservation of Nature and Natural Resources (IUCN), Morges, Switzerland, Occasional Paper 14.

Reichenbacher, F. W. 1990. Tumamoc globe-berry studies in Arizona and Sonora, Mexico. U.S. Bureau of Reclamation Phoenix Office Contract Report BR8802-FR.

Reichenbacher, F. W., S. E. Franson, and D. E. Brown. 1998. Biotic communities of North America. University of Utah Press, Salt Lake City, Utah. Map (scale 1:10,000,000).

Ricketts, T., E. Dinerstein, D. M. Olson, C. Loucks, P. Hedao, K. Carney, S. Walters, and P. Hurley. 1997. Terrestrial ecoregions of the United States and Canada. World Wildlife Fund—U.S. Conservation Science Program and World Wildlife Fund, Canada. Map (scale 1:10,000.000).

Robbins, C. S., B. Bruun, and H. S. Zim. 1966. Birds of North America: a guide to field identification. Golden Press, New York.

Rowe, J. S. 1972. Forest regions of Canada. Canadian Forest Service Publication, Number 1300. Information Canada, Ottawa.

Ruthven, A. G. 1920. The environmental factors in the distribution of animals. Geographical Review 10:241–48.

Ryan, R. M. 1963. The biotic provinces of Central America. Acta Zoologica Mexicana 6:1–54.

Rzedowski, J. 1978. Vegetación de México. Editorial Limusa S. A., Mexico, D.F.

Sclater, P. L. 1858. On the general geographical distribution of the members of the class Aves. Journal and Proceedings of the Linnean Society (Zoology) 2:130–45.

Sclater, P. L., and W. L. Sclater. 1889. The geography of mammals. Kegan, Paul, Trench, Trübner, and Co., London.

Shantz, H. L., and R. Zön. 1924. Natural vegetation. Atlas of American agriculture. Plot 1, Section E. Map. U.S. Department of Agriculture, Washington, D.C.

Sharpe, R. B. 1893. On the zoo-geographical areas of the world, illustrating the distribution of birds. Natural Sciences 3:100–108.

Shelford, V. E. 1932a. Life-zones, modern ecology, and the failure of tem-perature summing. Wilson Bulletin 44:144–57.

———. 1932b. A nature sanctuary plan unanimously adopted by the Society, December 28, 1932. Ecology 14:240–45.

———. 1945. The relative merits of the life zone and biome concepts. Wilson Bulletin 57:248–52.

———. 1963. The ecology of North America. University of Illinois Press, Urbana, Illinois.

Shreve, F. 1917. A map of the vegetation of the United States. Geographical Review 3:119–25.

———. 1942. The desert vegetation of North America. Botanical Review 8:195–246.

———. 1951. Vegetation and flora of the Sonoran Desert. Volume 1, Vegetation. Carnegie Institution of Washington Publication 591.

Simpson, G. G. 1961. Principles of animal taxonomy. Columbia University Press, New York.

———. 1964. Species density of North American recent mammals. Systematic Zoology 13:57–73.

Sims, P. L. 1988. Grasslands. P. 265–286. In North American terrestrial vegetation, M. G. Barbour and W. D. Billings, eds. Cambridge University Press, Cambridge.

Society of American Foresters. 1954. Forest cover types of North America (exclusive of Mexico). Society of American Foresters, Washington, D.C.

Stacey, R., and J. Knighton. 1994. North America From Space. 1:13,200,000. World Sat Intern., Inc., Mississauga, Ontario, and Replogle Globes, Inc., Broadview, Illinois.

Stejneger, L., and G. S. Miller, Jr. 1903. Plan for a biological survey of the Palearctic Region. Carnegie Institution of Washington Yearbook 1:240–66.

Sterling, K. B. 1974. Selections from the literature of American biogeogra-phy. Arno Press, New York.

———. 1977. Last of the naturalists: the career of C. H. Merriam. Revised edition. Arno Press, New York.

Takhtajan, A. 1986. The floristic regions of the world. University of California Press, Berkeley.

Tansley, A. G. 1923. Practical plant ecology: a guide for beginners in field study of plant communities. Allen and Unwin, London.

Tharp, B. C. 1939. The vegetation of Texas. Texas Academy Publications in Natural History 1. Published for the Texas Academy of Science by the Anson Jones Press, Houston.

Tosi, J. A., Jr. 1969. República de Costa Rica, mapa ecológico. Centro Científico Tropical, San José, Costa Rica. Map (scale 1:750,000).

Turner, R. M. 1982. Mohave Desertscrub. In Biotic communities of the American Southwest: United States and Mexico, D. E. Brown, ed., 157–68. Desert Plants 4(1–4).

Udvardy, M. D. F. 1969. Dynamic zoogeography, with special reference to land animals. Van Nostrand Reinhold, New York.

———. 1975a. World biogeographical provinces. CoEvolution Quarterly, Sausalito. Map (scale 1:39,629,000).

———. 1975b. A classification of the biogeographical provinces of the world. International Union for Conservation of Nature and Natural Resources (IUCN), Morges, Switzerland. Paper Number 18.

———. 1984a. The IUCN/UNESCO system of biogeographical provinces in relation to the biosphere reserves. In Conservation, sciences and so-ciety: contribution to the First International Biosphere Reserve

Congress, Minsk, Byelorussia/U.S.S.R, 26 Sept.–2 Oct., 1983, 16–19. UNESCO-UNEP.

———. 1984b. A biogeographical classification system for terrestrial environments. In National parks, conservation and development: the role of protected areas in sustaining society. Proceedings of the World Congress on National Parks, Bali, Indonesia, 11–22 October 1982, J. A. McNeely and K. R. Miller, eds., 34–38. Smithsonian Institution Press, Washington, D.C.

———. 1987. The biogeographical realm Antarctica: a proposal. In Forum on the biogeographical classifications of New Zealand. Journal of the Royal Society of New Zealand 17:187–200.

U.S. Department of Agriculture, Soil Conservation Service. 1975. Soil taxonomy: a basic system of soil classification for making and interpreting soil surveys. U.S. Government Printing Office, Washington, D.C. Agriculture Handbook Number 436.

U.S. Department of Interior, Federal Geographic Data Committee. 1995. Draft FGDC vegetation standards (revised).

Vestal, A. G. 1914. Internal relations of terrestrial associations. American Naturalist 48:413–45.

Wallace, A. R. 1876. The geographical distribution of animals, with a study of the relations of living and extinct faunas as elucidating the past changes of the earth's surface. 2 volumes. MacMillan and Company, London.

Walter, H. 1973. Vegetation of the earth in relation to climate and the ecophysiological conditions. Translated from the Second German Edition by Joy Wieser. English Universities Press, London; Springer-Verlag, New York.

Warming, E. 1909. Oecology of plants: an introduction to the study of plant communities. The Clarendon Press, Oxford.

Weaver, J. E., and F. E. Clements. 1938. Plant ecology. Second edition. McGraw-Hill Book Company, Inc., New York.

Webb, W. L. 1950. Biogeographic regions of Texas and Oklahoma. Ecology 31:426–43.

Whittaker, R. H. 1962. Classification of natural communities. Botanical Review 28:1–239.

———, ed. 1978. Classification of plant communities. Dr. W. Junk, The Hague-Boston.

Wickware, G. M., and C. D. A. Rubec. 1989. Terrestrial ecoregions and ecodistricts of Ontario. Map (scale 1:2,000,000) and descriptive table. In Ecoregions of Ontario. Environment Canada, Lands Directorate, Ottawa, Ontario. Ecological Land Classification Series 26.

Wieslander, A. E. 1935. A vegetation type map of California. Madroño 3:140–44.

Wiken, E. B., compiler. 1986. Terrestrial ecozones of Canada. Environment Canada, Lands Directorate, Ottawa, Ontario. Ecological Land Classification Series 19.

Wiken, E. B., C. D. A. Rubec, and G. R. Ironside. 1989. Terrestrial ecoregions of Canada. Provisional map (scale 1:7,500,000). Environment Canada, Sustainable Development Branch, Ottawa, Ontario.

Wilson, J. W., III. 1974. Analytical zoogeography of North American mammals. Evolution 28:124–40.

Yang, T. W. 1970. Major chromosome races of Larrea divaricata in North America. Journal of the Arizona Academy of Science 6:41–45.

Zoltai, S. C., F. C. Pollett, J. K. Jeglum, and G. D. Adams. 1975. Developing a wetland classification for Canada. Proceedings of the North American Forest Soils Conference 4:497–511.

Literature Consulted

Aleksandrova, V. D. 1980. The arctic and antarctic, their division into geobotanical areas. (Translated by Doris Löve.) Cambridge University Press, Cambridge.

Archibold, O. W. 1995. Ecology of world vegetation. Chapman & Hall, London.

Asplund, K. K. 1967. Ecology of lizards in the relictual Cape flora, Baja California. American Midland Naturalist 77:462–75.

Asprey, G. F. 1960. Vegetation in the Caribbean area. Caribbean Quarterly 5.

Asprey, G. F., and R. G. Robbins. 1953. The vegetation of Jamaica. Ecological Monographs 23.

Austin, M. E. 1965. Land resource regions and major land resource areas of the United States, exclusive of Alaska and Hawaii. Agricultural Handbook 296. U.S. Department of Agriculture, Soil Conservation Service, Washington, D.C.

Bailey, V. 1905. Biological survey of Texas: life zones and characteristic species of mammals, birds, reptiles, and plants. North American Fauna 25. U.S. Department of Agriculture, Washington, D.C.

———. 1913. Life zones and crop zones of New Mexico. North American Fauna 35. U.S. Department of Agriculture, Washington, D.C.

———. 1926. A biological survey of North Dakota: I. Physiography and life zones. II. The mammals. North American Fauna 49. U.S. Department of Agriculture, Washington, D.C.

———. 1931. Mammals of New Mexico. North American Fauna 53. U.S. Department of Agriculture, Washington, D.C.

———. 1936. The mammals and life zones of Oregon. North American Fauna 55. U.S. Department of Agriculture, Washington, D.C.

Bancroft, G. 1926. The faunal areas of Baja California del Norte. Condor 28:209–15.

Banks, R. C. 1967. Birds and mammals of La Laguna, Baja California. Transactions of the San Diego Society of Natural History 14:205–32.

Bauer, H. L. 1930. Vegetation of the Tehachapi Mountains, California. Ecology 11:263–80.

Beard, J. S. 1938. The natural vegetation of Trinidad. Oxford Forestry Memoirs 20.

———. 1942. Montane vegetation in the Antilles. Caribbean Forester 3:61–74.

———. 1944a. Climax vegetation in tropical America. Ecology 25:127–58.

———. 1944b. The natural vegetation of the island of Tobago, British West Indies. Ecological Monographs 14:140.

———. 1949. The natural vegetation of the Windward and Leeward Islands. Oxford Forestry Memoirs 21.

———. 1955. The classification of tropical America vegetation types. Ecology 36:89–100.

Beebe, W. 1952. Introduction to the ecology of the Arima Valley, Trinidad, B. W. I. Zoologica 37:158.

Bentley, J. R., and M. W. Talbot. 1948. Annual-plant vegetation of the California foothills as related to range management. Ecology 29:72–79.

Billings, W. D. 1945. The plant association of the Carson Desert region, western Nevada. Butler University Botanical Studies 7:89–123.

———. 1949. The shadscale vegetation zone of Nevada and eastern California in relation to climate and soils. American Midland Naturalist 42(1):87–109.

———. 1973. Arctic and alpine vegetations: similarities, differences, and susceptibility to disturbance. BioScience 23:697–704.

———. 1979. Alpine ecosystems of western North America. In Special management needs of alpine ecosystems, D. A. Johnson, ed., 6–21. Society Range Management, Denver, Colorado.

———. 1988. Alpine vegetation. In North American terrestrial vegetation, M. G. Barbour and W. D. Billings, eds., 391–420.Cambridge University Press, Cambridge.

Biswell, H. H. 1956. Ecology of California grasslands. Journal of Range Management 9:19–24.

Bliss, L. C. 1963. The alpine plant communities of the Presidential Range, New Hampshire. Ecology 44:678–97.

———. 1975. Tundra grasslands, herblands, and shrublands and the role of herbivores. Geoscience and Man 10:51–79.

———. 1981. North American and Scandinavian tundras and polar deserts. In Tundra ecosystems: a comparative analysis, L. C. Bliss, O. W. Heal, and J. J. Moore, eds., 8–24. Cambridge University Press, Cambridge.

Böcher, T. W. 1954. Oceanic and continental vegetational complexes in southwest Greenland. C. A. Reitzel, København. Meddelelser om Grønland 148(1).

———. 1963. Phytogeography of middle west Greenland. C. A. Reitzel, København, Meddelelser om Grønland 148(3).

Bougeron, P. S., and L. D. Engelking, eds. 1994. A preliminary vegetation classification of the western United States. Unpublished Report. The Nature Conservancy Western Heritage Task Force, Boulder, Colorado.

Bourdeau, P. F., and H. J. Oosting. 1959. The maritime liveoak forest in North Carolina. Ecology 40:148–52.

Bradley, J. T. 1972. Climate of Florida. U.S. Department of Commerce, National Oceanic and Atmospheric Administration, Environmental Data Services. Climatography of the United States, No. 60-B.

Brand, D. D. 1936. Notes to accompany a vegetation map of northwestern Mexico. University of New Mexico Bulletin, Biological Series 4:5–27.

Brassard, G. R., and R. E. Longton. 1970. The flora and vegetation of Van Hauen Pass, northwestern Ellesmere Island. Canadian Field-Naturalist 84:357–64.

Bray, J. R. 1960. The composition of savanna vegetation in Wisconsin. Ecology 41:721–32.

Breedlove, D. E. 1981. Introduction to the flora of Chiapas. In The Flora of Chiapas. California Academy of Sciences.

Bromley, S. W. 1935. The original forest types of southern New England. Ecological Monographs 5:61–89.

Brown, D. M. 1941. The vegetation of Roan Mountain. Ecological Monographs 11:61–97.

Brown, R. T., and J. T. Curtis. 1952. The upland conifer-hardwood forests of northern Wisconsin. Ecological Monographs 22:217–34.

Bryant, J. P., and E. Scheinberg. 1970. Vegetation and frost activity in an alpine fellfield on the summit of Plateau Mountain, Alberta. Canadian Journal of Botany 48:751–71.

Buechner, H. K. 1946. Birds of Kerr County, Texas. Transactions of the Kansas Academy of Science 49:357–64.

Buell, M. F., and W. E. Gordon. 1945. Hardwood-conifer contact zone in Itasca Park, Minnesota. American Midland Naturalist 34:433–39.

Buell, M. F., and W. F. Niering. 1957. Fir-spruce-birch forest in southern Minnesota. Ecology 38:602–10.

Burcham, L. T. 1956. Historical background of range landuse in California. Journal of Range Management 9:81–86.

Cabrera, A.L., and A. Willink. 1980. Biogeografiá de América Latina. Organisación de Estados Americanos, Washington, D.C.

Cameron, J. 1929. The Bureau of Biological Survey: its history, activities and organization. Institution for Government Research Service, Monographs of the United States Government 54. John Hopkins Press, Baltimore.

Canadian Forest Service. 1949. Native trees of Canada. Fourth edition. Department of Mines and Resources; Mines, Forests and Scientific Service Branch; Dominion Forest Service; Ottawa. Forest Service Bulletin 61.

Carabia, J. T. 1945. Vegetation of Sierra de Nipa, Cuba. Ecological Monographs 15:321–34.

Carpenter, R. J. 1940. The grassland biome. Ecological Monographs 10:618–84.

Cary, M. 1911. A biological survey of Colorado. North American Fauna 33. U.S. Department of Agriculture, Washington, D.C.

———. 1917. Life-zone investigations in Wyoming. North American Fauna 42. U.S. Department of Agriculture, Washington, D.C.

Castetter, E. F. 1956. The vegetation of New Mexico. New Mexico Quarterly 26:257–88.

Chabot, B. F., and W. D. Billings. 1972. Origins and ecology of the Sierran alpine flora and vegetation. Ecological Monographs 42:163–99.

Chapman, J. A., and J. E. C. Flux, eds. 1990. Rabbits, hares and pikas: status survey and conservation action plan. International Union for Conservation of Nature and Natural Resources, Gland, Switzerland.

Clokey, I. W. 1951. Flora of the Charleston Mountains, Clark County, Nevada. University of California Publications in Botany 24. University of California Press, Berkeley.

Clover, E. U. 1937. Vegetational survey of the lower Rio Grande Valley, Texas. Madroño 4:41–66, 77–100.

Colinvaux, P. A. 1964. The environment of the Bering land bridge. Ecological Monographs 34:297–329.

Comisión Técnico Consultiva Para La Determinación Regional De Los Coeficientes De agostadero. 1974. Tipos de Vegetación en el Estado de Sonora (maps). In Coeficientes De Agostadero de la República Mexicana, Estado de Sonora. Secretaria de Agricultura Y Ganaderia, Mexico, D.F.

Corns, I. G. W. 1974. Arctic plant communities east of the Mackenzie Delta. Canadian Journal of Botany 52:1730–45.

Correll, D. S. 1979. The Bahama Archipelago and its plant communities. Taxon 28:35–40.

Cottle, H. J. 1931. Studies on the vegetation of southwestern Texas. Ecology 12:105–55.

———. 1932. Vegetation on north and south slopes of mountains in southwestern Texas. Ecology 13:121–34.

Critchfield, W. B., and E. L. Little, Jr. 1966. Geographic distribution of the pines of the world. U.S. Department of Agriculture, Forest Service, Miscellaneous Publication number 991. Washington, D.C.

Cronemiller, F. P. 1942. Chaparral. Madroño 6:199–200.

Curtis, J. T. 1959. The vegetation of Wisconsin: an ordination of plant communities. University of Wisconsin Press, Madison.

Daniels, F. J. A. 1982. Vegetation of the Angmagssalik District, Southeast Greenland. IV Shrub, dwarf shrub and terricolous lichens. Meddelelser om Grønland, Bioscience 10:1–78.

———. 1994. Considerations regarding a legend for a circumpolar arctic vegetation map (1:7,500,000 scale) based on Greenland experience. In Circumpolar arctic vegetation mapping workshop, D. A. Walker and C. J. Markon, eds., 8–93. Komarov Botanical Institute, St. Petersburg.

Dansereau, P. 1966. Studies on the vegetation of Puerto Rico, I. University of Puerto Rico Special Publication 1:1–45.

Dansereau, P., and F. P. Buell. 1966. Studies on the vegetation of Puerto Rico, II. University of Puerto Rico Special Publication 1:46–287.

Daubenmire, R. F. 1952. Forest vegetation of northern Idaho and adjacent Washington and its bearing on concepts of vegetation classification. Ecological Monographs 22:303–30.

———. 1953. Notes on vegetation of forested regions of the far northern Rockies and Alaska. Northwest Science 27:125–38.

———. 1969. Ecologic plant geography of the Pacific Northwest. Madroño 20:111–28.

———. 1970. Steppe vegetation of Washington. Washington Agricultural Experiment Station, Pullman, Technical Bulletin 62.

Davis, J. 1959. The Sierra Madrean element of the avifauna of the Cape district, Baja California. Condor 61:75–84.

Davis, J. H. 1942. The ecology of the vegetation and topography of the sand keys of Florida. Carnegie Institution of Washington Publication 524:113–95.

———. 1943. The natural features of southern Florida, especially the vegetation and the Everglades. Florida Geological Survey, Geological Bulletin 25.

Davis, R. B. 1966. Spruce-fir forests of the coast of Maine. Ecological Monographs 36:79–94.

Denevan, W. M. 1961. The upland pine forests of Nicaragua: a study in cultural plant geography. University of California Publications in Geography 124:251–320.

Detling, L. E. 1961. The chaparral formation of southwestern Oregon, with considerations of its postglacial history. Ecology 42:348–57.

Dice, L. R. 1931. The relation of mammalian distribution to vegetation types. Scientific Monthly 33:312–17.

Douglas, G. W., and L. C. Bliss. 1977. Alpine and high subalpine plant communities of the North Cascades Range, Washington and British Columbia. Ecological Monographs 47:113–50.

Duellman, W. E. 1966. The Central American herpetofauna: an ecological perspective. Copeia 700–719.

Dupree, A. H. 1957. Science in the federal government: a history of policies and activities to 1940. Belknap Press of Harvard University Press, Cambridge, Massachusetts.

Dyksterhuis, E. J. 1946. The vegetation of the Fort Worth prairie. Ecological Monographs 16:1–29.

———. 1948. The vegetation of the western Cross Timbers. Ecological Monographs 18:325–76.

Eggler, F. 1940. Bershire Plateau vegetation, Massachusetts. Ecological Monographs 10:145–92.

Elliot, D. L., and S. K. Short. 1979. The northern limit of trees in Laborador. Arctic 32:201–6.

Ellison, L. 1954. Subalpine vegetation of the Wasatch Plateau, Utah. Ecological Monographs 24:89–184.

Epling, C., and H. Lewis. 1942. The centers of distributions of the chaparral and coastal sage associations. American Midland Naturalist 27:445–62.

Etna, M. 1984. Le Climat de la Guadeloupe. CNDP, CDDP, Pointe-a-Pitre.

Everett, J. P. 1950. Latin America. Second edition, revised. Odyssey Press, New York.

Fautin, R. W. 1946. Biotic communities of the northern desert shrub biome in western Utah. Ecological Monographs 16:251–310.

Felger, R. S., and C. H. Lowe. 1976. The island and coastal vegetation and flora of the northern part of the Gulf of California. Natural History Museum of Los Angeles County Contributions in Science 285.

Fisher, A. K., L. Stejneger, C. V. Riley, R. E. C. Stearns, C. H. Merriam, and T. S. Palmer. 1893. The Death Valley Expedition: a biological survey of parts of California, Nevada, Arizona, and Utah. North American Fauna 7.

Fosberg, F. R. 1961. A classification of vegetation for general purposes. Tropical Ecology 2:1–28.

Friedman, S. 1996. Vegetation and flora of the coastal plains of the Rio Mayo region, southern Sonora, Mexico. M.S. thesis. Arizona State University, Tempe.

Gabriel, H. W., and S. S. Talbot. 1984. Glossary of landscape and vegetation ecology for Alaska. U.S. Department of the Interior, Bureau of Land Management, Alaska Technical Report 10.

Gentry, H. S. 1953. Los pastizales de Durango: estudio ecologico, fisiografico y floristico. Instituto Méxicano de Recursos Naturales Renovables, Mexico, D.F.

Gill, T. 1931. Tropical forests of the Caribbean. Tropical Plant Research Foundation in cooperation with the Charles Lathrop Pack Forestry Trust. U.S. Government Printing Office, Washington, D.C.

Golet, F. C., and J. S. Larson. 1974. Classification of fresh water wetlands in the glaciated Northeast. U.S. Department of the Interior, Bureau of Sport Fisheries and Wildlife, Fish and Wildlife Service, Research Publication 116.

Gomez-Pompa, A. 1978. Ecologia de la vegetación del estado de Veracruz. Compañia Editorial Continental, Mexico, D. F.

Graham, A., ed. 1973. Vegetation and vegetational history of northern Latin America. Papers presented as part of a symposium at the Institute of Biological Sciences meetings, Bloomington, Indiana, 1970. Elsevier Scientific Publishing Company, Amsterdam.

Grams, H. J., K. R. McPherson, V. V. King, S. A. MacLeod, and M. G. Barbour. 1977. Northern coastal scrub on Point Reyes Peninsula, California. Madroño 24:18–24.

Gregg, R. E. 1963. The ants of Colorado with reference to their ecology, taxonomy, and geographic distribution. University of Colorado Press, Boulder.

Griffin, J. R., and W. B. Critchfield. 1972. The distribution of forest trees in California. USDA Forest Service Research Paper PSW-82. Pacific Southwest Forest and Range Experiment Station, Berkeley, California.

Grinnell, J. 1928. A distributional summation of the ornithology of Lower California. University of California Publication in Zoology 32.

Griscom, L. 1932. The distribution of bird life in Guatemala. Bulletin of the American Museum of Natural History 64.

Hall, E. R. 1981. The mammals of North America. 2 volumes. John Wiley and Sons, New York.

Halliday, W. E. D., and A. W. A. Brown. 1943. The distribution of some important forest trees in Canada. Ecology 24:353–73.

Hansen, P. L., R. D. Pfister, K. Boggs, B. J. Cook, J. Joy, and D. K. Hinckley. 1995. Classification and management of Montana's riparian and wetland sites. Montana Forest and Conservation Experiment Station, School of Forestry, University of Montana, Missoula. Miscellaneous Publication 54.

Hanson, G. C. 1953. Vegetation types in northwestern Alaska and comparison with communities in other arctic regions. Ecology 34:111–40.

Hare, F. K. 1950. Climate and zonal divisions of the boreal forest formation in eastern Canada. Geographical Review 40:615–35.

Hare, F. K., and R. G. Taylor. 1956. The position of certain forest boundaries in southern Laborador-Ungava. Geographical Bulletin 8:51–73.

Harper, R. M. 1927. Natural resources of southern Florida. Florida State Geological Survey Annual Report 18:27–206.

Hayward, C. L. 1952. Alpine biotic communities in the Uintah Mountains, Utah. Ecological Monographs 22:93–120.

Heady, H. F., T. C. Foin, M. M. Hektner, D. W. Taylor, M. G. Barbour, and W. J. Barry. 1977. Coastal prairie and northern coastal scrub. In Terrestrial vegetation of California, M. G. Barbour and J. Major, eds. 733–60. 1988. Second edition. California Native Plant Society Special Publication 9.

Hodge, W. H. 1941. The vegetation of the Lesser Antilles, a brief review. Chronica Botanica 6.

Holdridge, L. R. 1940. Some notes on mangrove swamps of Puerto Rico. Caribbean Forester 1:19–30.

Holttum, R. E. 1922. The vegetation of west Greenland. Journal of Ecology 10:87–108.

Hopkins, D. M. 1959. Some characteristics of the climate in forest and tundra regions in Alaska. Arctic 12:215–20.

Howard, R. A. 1950. Vegetation of the Bimini Island group, Bahamas. Ecological Monographs 20:317–49.

———. 1962. Volcanism and vegetation in the Lesser Antilles. Journal of the Arnold Arboretum 43:279–314.

———. 1968. The ecology of an elfin forest in Puerto Rico. I. Introduction and composition studies. Journal of the Arnold Arboretum 49:381–418.

Howell, A. H. 1921. A biological survey of Alabama. North American Fauna 45.

Howell, S. N. G., and S. Webb. 1994. A guide to the birds of Mexico and northern Central America. Oxford University Press, Oxford.

Hubbs, C. L., ed. 1958. Zoogeography. American Association for the Advancement of Science. Publication Number 51.

Hunter, J. R. 1959. Limites climaticos del cacao, café, y hule. Instit. Interamericano de Ciencias Agricolas, Materiales de ense–anza de café y cacao, 16E. Turrialba, Costa Rica.

Hurd, R. M. 1961. Grassland vegetation in the Bighorn Mountains, Wyoming. Ecology 42:459–67.

Hustich, I. 1953. The boreal limits of conifers. Arctic 6:149–62.

———. 1962. A comparison of the floras of subarctic mountains of Labrador and in Finnish Lapland. Acta Geographica 17:1–24.

Isard, S. A. 1986. Factors influencing soil moisture and plant community distributions on Niwot Ridge, Front Range, Colorado, U.S.A. Arctic and Alpine Research 18:83–96.

Ives, J. D., and R. G. Berry, eds. 1974. Arctic and alpine environments. Methuen, London.

Jeffries, R. L. 1977. The vegetation of salt marshes at some coastal sites in arctic North America. Journal of Ecology 65:661–72.

Johannessen, C. L. 1963. Savannas of interior Honduras. Ibero-Americana 46.

———. 1971. The vegetation of the Willamette Valley. Annals of the Association of American Geographers 61:286–302.

Johnson, P. L., and W. D. Billings. 1962. The alpine vegetation of the Beartooth Plateau in relation to cryopedogenic processes and patterns. Ecological Monographs 32:105–35.

Kershaw, K. A. 1976. The vegetation zonation of the East Pen Island salt marshes, Hudson Bay. Canadian Journal of Botany 54:5–13.

Kevan, P. 1972. Insect pollination of high arctic flowers. Journal of Ecology 60:831–47.

Knight, H. D. 1975. A phylosociological analysis of species-rich tropical forest on Barro Colorado Island, Panama. Ecological Monographs 45:259–84.

Komarkova, V. 1980. Classification and ordination in the Indian Peaks area, Colorado Rocky Mountains. Vegetation 42:149–63.

Komarkova, V., and P. J. Webber. 1978. An alpine vegetation map of Niwot Ridge, Colorado. Arctic and Alpine Research 10:1–29.

Krajina, V. J. 1965. Biogeoclimatic zones and biogeocoenoses of British Columbia. In Ecology of western Northern America. University of British Columbia, Department of Botany, Vancouver.

Krizman, R. D. 1972. Environment and season in a tropical deciduous forest in northwestern Mexico. Ph.D. dissertation. University of Arizona, Tucson.

Krume, K. W. O., and C. B. Briscoe. 1963. Forest formations of Puerto Rico. Caribbean Forester 24:57–65.

Kuc, M. 1974. Noteworthy vascular plants collected in southwestern Banks Island, N.W.T. Arctic 26:146–50.

Küchler, A. W. 1946. The broadleaf deciduous forests of the Pacific Northwest. Annals of the Association of American Geographers 36:122–47.

Kuenhast, E. L. 1972. Climate of Minnesota. U.S. Department of Commerce, National Oceanic and Atmospheric Administration, Environmental Data and Information Service, National Climatic Center. Climatography of the United States No. 60-21.

La Roi, G. H. 1967. Ecological studies in the boreal spruce-fir forests of the North American taiga. Ecological Monographs 27:229–53.

Larsen, J. A. 1965. The vegetation of the Ennadai Lake area, N.W.T.: studies in subarctic and arctic bioclimatology. Ecological Monographs 35:37–59.

———. 1971. Vegetation of Fort Reliance, Northwest Territories. Canadian Field-Naturalist 85:147–78.

———. 1972. The vegetation of northern Keewatin. Canadian Field-Naturalist 86:45–72.

———. 1973. Plant communities north of the forest border, Keewatin, Northwest Territories. Canadian Field-Naturalist 87:241–48.

———. 1980. The boreal ecosystem. Academic Press, New York.

Lasserre, G. 1961. La Guadeloupe, etude geographie. Union Francaise d' Impression, Bordeaux, France.

Lautzenheizer, R. E. 1972. Climate of Maine. U.S. Department of Commerce, National Oceanic and Atmospheric Administration, Environmental Data and Information Service. Climatography of the United States No. 60-17.

Lawton, R. and V. Dryer. 1980. The vegetation of the Monteverde Cloud Forest Reserve. Brensia 18:101–16.

Lea, R. B., and E. P. Edwards. 1950. Notes on birds of the Lake Patzcuaro region, Michoacan, Mexico. Condor 52:260–71.

Leavenworth, W. C. 1946. A preliminary study of the vegetation of the region between Cerro Tancitaro and the Rio Tepalcatepec, Michoacan, Mexico. American Midland Naturalist 36:137–206.

Leopold, A. S. 1950. Vegetation zones of Mexico. Ecology 31:507–18.

LeSueur, H. D. 1945. The ecology of the vegetation of Chihuahua, Mexico, north of parallel twenty-eight. University of Texas Publication 452.

Little, E. L. 1941. Alpine flora of San Francisco Mountain, Arizona. Madroño 6:65–81.

———. 1950. Southwestern trees, a guide to the native species of New Mexico and Arizona. U.S. Department of Agriculture, Forest Service, Southwestern Forest and Range Experiment Station, Research Report Number 8.

Livingston, R. B. 1952. Relict true prairie communities in central Colorado. Ecology 33:72–86.

Lloyd, R. M., and R. S. Mitchell. 1973. A flora of the White Mountains, California and Nevada. University of California Press, Berkeley.

Longley, R. 1972. The climate of the Prairie Provinces. Canada Department of Environment, Atmospheric and Environmental Services, Climatological Studies 13.

Longstaff, A. S. 1932. An ecological reconnaissance in West Greenland. Journal of Animal Ecology 1:119–42.

Loope, L. L. 1969. Subalpine and alpine vegetation of northeastern Nevada. Ph.D. dissertation, Duke University, Durham, North Carolina.

Loveless, C. M. 1959. A study of the vegetation in the Florida Everglades. Ecology 40:1–9.

Loveless, A. R. 1960. The vegetation of Antigua, W. Indies. Journal of Ecology 48:495–527.

Loveless, A. R., and G. F. Asprey. 1957. The dry evergreen formations of Jamaica, W.I. Journal of Ecology 45:799–822.

Lowe, C. H., Jr. 1961. Biotic communities in the sub-Mogollon region of the inland Southwest. Journal of the Arizona Academy of Science 2:40–49.

Lundell, C. L. 1934. A preliminary sketch of the phytogeography of the Yucatán Peninsula. Carnegie Institution of Washington Publication 436:257–355.

———. 1937. The vegetation of Petén. Carnegie Institution of Washington Publication 436:1–244.

———. 1966. Vegetation of the arctic tundra. In Arctic Biology, H. P. Hansen, ed. Second Edition. Oregon State University Press, Corvallis.

Lynch, D. 1962. Study of a grassland mosaic at Austin, Texas. Ecology 43:679–86.

MacArthur, R. H. 1964. Environmental factors affecting bird species diversity. American Naturalist 98:387–98.

MacIntosh, R. P., and R. T. Hurley. 1966. The spruce-fir forests of the Catskill Mountains. Ecology 45:314–26.

Macnae, W. 1968. A general account of the fauna and flora of mangrove swamps and forests in the Indo-West Pacific region. Advances in Marine Biology 6:73–270.

Major, J., and D. W. Taylor. 1977. Alpine. In Terrestrial vegetation of California, M. G. Barbour and J. Major, eds., 601–75. 1977. John Wiley and Sons, New York.

Martin, P. S. 1955. Zonal distribution of vertebrates in a Mexican cloud forest. American Midland Naturalist 89:347–61.

Martin, P. S., C. R. Robins, and W. B. Head. 1954. Birds and biogeography of the Sierra de Tamaulipas, an isolated oak-pine habitat. Wilson Bulletin 66:38–57.

Maycock, P. F. 1961. The spruce-fir forests of the Keweenaw Peninsula, northern Michigan. Ecology 42:357–65.

———. 1963. The phytosociology of the deciduous forests of extreme southern Ontario. Canadian Journal of Botany 41:379–438.

McNaughton, S. J. 1968. Structure and function in California grasslands. Ecology 49:962–72.

Merkle, J. 1962. Plant communities of the Grand Canyon area, Arizona. Ecology 43:698–711.

Merriam, C. H. 1899. Results of a biological survey of Mount Shasta, California. North American Fauna 16.

———. 1935. The biological survey—origin and early days—a retrospect. The Survey. March:39–43.

Merriam, C. H., and L. Stejneger. 1891. Results of a biological reconnaissance of south-central Idaho. North American Fauna 5.

Miller, P. C., ed. 1982. The availability and utilization of resources in tundra ecosystems. Holarctic Ecology 5:81–220.

Mills, G. F., H. Veldhuis, and D. B. Forrester. 1978. A guide to biophysical land classification. Manitoba Department of Renewable Resources and Transportation Services, Canada-Manitoba Soil Survey for Province of Manitoba, Winnipeg, Manitoba. Technical Report 78-7.

Mirov, N. T., and E. Larsen. 1958. Possibilities of Mexican and Central American pines in the world reforestation projects. Caribbean Forester 19:46.

Mooney, H. A. 1973. Plant communities and vegetation. In A flora of the White Mountains, California and Nevada. R. M. Lloyd and R. S. Mitchell. University of California Press, Berkeley.

Moore, R. T. 1945. The transverse volcanic biotic province of Central Mexico and its relationship to adjacent provinces. Transactions of the San Diego Society of Natural History 10:217–35.

Moss, E. H. 1953. Forest communities in northwest Alberta. Canadian Journal of Botany 31:212–52.

———. 1955. The vegetation of Alberta. Botanical Review 21:493–567.

Muller, C. H. 1937. Vegetation in Chisos Mountains, Texas. Transactions of the Texas Academy of Sciences 20:5–31.

———. 1939. Relations of the vegetation and climatic types in Nuevo Leon, Mexico. American Midland Naturalist 21:687–729.

Nelson, E. W. 1921. Lower California and its natural resources. Memoirs of the National Academy of Sciences 16.

Nelson, E. W., L. Stejneger, M. J. Athbun, and J. N. Rose. 1899. Natural history of the Tres Marias Islands, Mexico. North American Fauna 14.

Nichols, G. E. 1935. The hemlock-white pine northern hardwoods region of eastern North America. Ecology 16:403–22.

Nothop, A. R. 1902. Flora of New Providence and Andros, Bahama Islands. Memoirs of the Torrey Botanical Club 12.

Oosting, H. J. 1948. Ecological notes on the flora of east Greenland and Jan Mayen. In The coast of northeast Greenland, L. A. Boyd, ed., 225–69. 1948. American Geographical Society Special Publication 30.

Oosting, H. J., and W. D. Billings. 1951. A comparison of virgin spruce-fir forest in the northern and southern Appalachian system. Ecology 32:84–103.

Oosting, H. J., and J. F. Reed. 1952. Virgin spruce-fir forest in the Medicine Bow Mountains, Wyoming. Ecological Monographs 22:69–91.

Orr, R. T. 1960. An analysis of the recent land mammals. In The biogeography of Baja California and adjacent seas. Systematic Zoology 9:171–79.

Osgood, W. H. 1900. Results of a biological reconnaissance of the Yukon region. North American Fauna 19.

———. 1901. Natural history of the Queen Charlotte Islands, British Columbia; and natural history of the Cook Inlet region, Alaska. North American Fauna 21.

———. 1904. A biological reconnaissance of the base of the Alaska Peninsula. North American Fauna 24.

———. 1909. Biological investigations in Alaska and Yukon Territory. North American Fauna 30.

Parker, J. 1952. Environment and forest distribution of the Palouse Range in northern Idaho. Ecology 33:451–61.

Parsons, J. J. 1955. The Miskito pine savanna of Nicaragua and Honduras. Annals of the Association of American Geographers 45:36–63.

Penfound, W. T. 1952. Southern swamps and marshes. Botanical Review 18:413–46.

Polunin, N.V. 1948. Botany of the Canadian eastern Arctic. Part III. Vegetation and ecology. National Museum of Canada Bulletin 104, Ottawa.

Polunin, O., and M. Walters. 1985. A guide to the vegetation of Britain and Europe. Oxford University Press, Oxford.

Preble, E. A. 1902. A biological investigaion of the Hudson Bay region. North American Fauna 22.

———. 1908. A biological investigation of the Athabaska-Mackenzie region. North American Fauna 27.

Preble, E. A., and W. L. McAtee. 1923. A biological survey of the Pribilof Islands, Alaska. North American Fauna 46.

Quarterman, E., and C. Keaver. 1962. Southern mixed hardwood forest: climax in the southern coastal plain, U.S.A. Ecological Monographs 32:167–85.

Randall, E. R. 1970. Vegetation and environment on the Barbados coast. Journal of Ecology 58:155–72.

Raup, H. M. 1946. Phytogeographic studies in the Athbasca-Great Slave Lake region, II. Journal of the Arnold Arboretum 27:1–85.

Redington, P. 1933. The U.S. Biological Survey. Scientific Monthly October:289–306.

Reznicek, S. A., and J. Svoboda. 1982. Tundra communities along a microenvironmental gradient at Coral Harbour, Southampton Island, N.W.T. Naturaliste Canadien 109:585–95.

Rice, K. A. 1971. Climate of Idaho. U.S. Department of Commerce, National Oceanic and Atmospheric Administration, Environmental Data and Information Service. Climatography of the United States No. 60-10.

Ritchie, J. C. 1960. The vegetation of northern Manitoba. V. Establishing the major zonation. Arctic 13:211–29.

———. 1983. Past and present vegetation of the far northwest of Canada. Toronto University Press, Toronto.

Ross, P. 1961. The plant ecology of the teak plantations in Trinidad. Ecology 42:389.

Sawyer, J. O., and A. A. Lindsey. 1971. Vegetation of the life zones of Costa Rica. Indiana Academy of Science Monograph 2.

Sawyer, J. O., and T. Keeler-Wolf. 1995. A manual of California vegetation. California Native Plant Society.

Schaak, C. G. 1983. The alpine vascular flora of Arizona. Madroño 30:79–88.

Schmidt, K. P. 1942. A cloud forest camp in Honduras. Chicago Naturalist 5:23–30.

———. 1946. On the zoogeography of the Holarctic region. Copeia: 144–52.

Schmidt, R. H., Jr. 1979. A climatic delineation of the "real" Chihuahuan Desert. Journal of Arid Environments 2:243–50.

Scott, G. A. J. 1995. Canada's vegetation: a world perspective. McGill-Queen's University Press, Montreal.

Seifriz, W. 1943. The plant life of Cuba. Ecological Monographs 13:375–426.

Sheard, J. W., and D. W. Geale. 1983. Vegetation studies of Polar Bear Pass, Bathurst Island, N. W. T. I. Classification of plant communities. Canadian Journal of Botany 61:1618–36.

Shelford, V. E. 1954. Some lower Mississippi valley floodplain biotic communities: their age and elevations. Ecology 35:126–42.

Shelford, V. E., and F. Shreve, eds. 1926. Naturalist's guide to the Americas. Williams and Wilkins, Baltimore.

Shreve, F. 1934. Vegetation of the northwestern coast of Mexico. Bulletin of the Torrey Botanical Club 61:373–80.

———. 1936. The transition from desert to chaparral in Baja California. Madroño 3:257–64.

———. 1937a. The vegetation of Sinaloa. Bulletin of the Torrey Botanical Club 64:605–13.

———. 1937b. The vegetation of the cape region of Baja California. Madroño 4:105–13.

———. 1939. Observations on the vegetation of Chihuahua. Madroño 5:1–13.

———. 1942. Grassland and related vegetation in northern Mexico. Madroño 6:190–98.

———. 1944. Rainfall of northern Mexico. Ecology 25:105–11.

Sigafoos, R. S. 1958. Vegetation of northwestern North America. United States Geological Survey Bulletin 1061:165–85.

Slud, P. 1960. The birds of Finca "La Selva," Costa Rica: a tropical wet forest locality. American Museum of Natural History Bulletin 121:53–148.

———. 1964. The birds of Costa Rica: distribution and ecology. American Museum of Natural History Bulletin 128.

Smith, E. S. 1954. The forests of Cuba. Maria Moors Cabot Foundation (in cooperation with Howard Forest Petersham, Massachusetts, and Aatkins Garden and Research Laboratory, Cienfuegos, Cuba) Publication 2.

Spetzman, L. A. 1959. Vegetation of the Arctic Slope of Alaska. U.S. Geological Survey Professional Paper 302-B. Washington, D.C.

St. Andre, G. H., H. A. Mooney, and R. C. Wright. 1965. The pinyon woodland zone in the White Mountains of California. American Midland Naturalist 73:225–39.

Steele, R., R. D. Pfister, R. A. Ryker, and J. A. Kittans. 1981. Forest habitat types of central Idaho. U.S. Department of Agriculture, Forest Service, Inter-mountain Forest and Range Experiment Station, General Technical Report INT-114.

Stehlé, H. 1945. Forest types of the Caribbean Islands. Part I. Caribbean Forester 6 (Supplement): 273–422.

———. 1946. Vegetation districts in Martinique. Caribbean Forester 6.

Stiles, F. G., and A. F. Skutch. 1989. A guide to the birds of Costa Rica. Comstock, Ithaca.

Stoddart, L. A. 1941. The palouse grassland association in northern Utah. Ecology 22:349–475.

Strong, W. L., E. T. Oswald, and D. J. Downing, eds. 1990. The Canadian vegetation classification system. Ecological Land Classification Series 25:1–22.

Stuart, L. C. 1954. A description of a subhumid corridor across northern Central America, with comments on its herpetological indicators. Contributions from the Laboratory of Vertebrate Biology, University of Michigan 65:1–26.

Talbot, M. W., H. H. Biswell, and A. L. Hormay. 1949. Fluctuations in the annual vegetation of California. Ecology 20:394–402.

Tanner, E. V. J. 1977. Four montane rainforests of Jamaica. Journal of Ecology 65:883–918.

Tans, W. 1976. The presettlement vegetation of Columbia County, Wisconsin in the 1830's. Wisconsin Department of Natural Resources Technical Bulletin 90.

Taylor, B. W. 1963. An outline of the vegetation of Nicaragua. Journal of Ecology 51:27–54.

Taylor, R. A. 1967. A tropical hammock on the Miami (Florida) limestone—a twenty-five year study. Ecology 48:863–67.

Taylor, R. L., and B. MacBryde. 1977. Vascular plants of British Columbia: a descriptive resource inventory. University of British Columbia Press, Vancouver.

Thilenius, F. 1968. The *Quercus garryana* forests of the Willamette Valley, Oregon. Ecology 49:1124–33.

Thomas, M. K. 1953. Climatological atlas of Canada. Natural Resources Council of Canada, Division of Building Research, Ottawa. NRC 3151.

Thompson, D. C. 1980. A classification of the vegetation of Boothia Peninsula and northern district of Keewatin, N.W.T. Arctic 33:73–99.

Tisdale, E. W. 1947. The grasslands of the southern interior of British Columbia. Ecology 28:346–82.

Turner, R. M., J. E. Bowers, and T. L. Burgess. 1995. Sonoran desert plants: an ecological atlas. University of Arizona Press, Tucson.

Verdoorn, F., ed. 1945. Plants and plant science in Latin America. Chronica Botanica Company, Waltham, Massachusetts.

Vestergaard, P. 1978. Studies in vegetation and soil of coastal salt marshes in the Disko area, west Greenland. Meddelelser om Grønland 204.

Viereck, L. A., and E. L. Little, Jr. 1972. Alaska trees and shrubs. U.S. Department of Agriculture, Forest Service, Washington, D.C. Agriculture Handbook 410.

Viereck, L. A., C. T. Dyrness, A. R. Batten, and K. J. Wenzlick. 1992. The Alaska vegetation classification. U.S. Department of Agriculture, Forest Service, Pacific Northwest Research Station, Portland, Oregon. General Technical Report PNW-GTR-286.

Vogl, R. J., and B. C. Miller. 1968. The vegetational composition of the south slope of Mt. Pinos, California. Madroño 19:225–34.

Warren Wilson, J. 1959. Notes on wind and its effects on arctic-alpine vegetation. Journal of Ecology 47:415–27.

Watts, F. B. 1960. The natural vegetation of the southern Great Plains of Canada. Geographical Bulletin 14:25–43.

Weaver, J. E., and W. E. Bruner. 1948. Prairies and pastures of the dissected loess plains of central Nebraska. Ecological Monographs 18:507–49.

Webster, G. L. 1961. The altitudinal limits of vascular plants. Ecology 42:587–90.

Wein, R. W. 1976. Frequency and characteristics of arctic tundra fires. Arctic 29:213–22.

Westveld, M. 1956. Natural forest vegetation zones of New England. Journal of Forestry 54:332–38.

White, K. L. 1967. Native bunch grass (*Stipa pulchra*) on Hastings Reservation, California. Ecology 48:949–55.

White, S. S. 1949. The vegetation and flora of the region of the Rio de Bavispe in northeastern Sonora, Mexico. Lloydia 11(4):229–302.

Wilbur, S. R. 1987. Birds of Baja California. University of California Press, Berkeley.

Wilson, R. C., and R. J. Vogl. 1965. Manzanita chaparral in the Santa Ana Mountains, California. Madroño 18:47–62.

Wright, A. C. S. 1960. British Honduras natural vegetation. Map in color. British Honduras Survey Department, Belize City, Honduras. Map (scale 1:250,000).

Wright, A. H., and A. A. Wright. 1932. The habitats and the composition of the vegetation of Okeefinokee Swamp, Georgia. Ecological Monographs 2:190–232.

Wright, J. C. and E. A. Wright. 1948. Grassland types of south-central Montana. Ecology 9:449–60.

About the Authors   David Brown is an adjunct professor in the department of biology, Arizona State University.

Frank Reichenbacher, Ph.D., is an independent contractor with Southwest Field Biologists, Phoenix.

Susan Franson, Ph.D., works for the U.S. Environmental Protection Agency at the National Exposure Research Laboratory, Las Vegas.